15 Doors to Global Issues

Shinya Kawahara   Kenichiro Ito

Asahi Press

A 20th-century hero and icon from "The Japan Times 10/12/13"
Copyright © 2013 by The Japan Times Co. Reprinted with Permission

From Seaspeak to Singlish: celebrating other kings of English by Rosie Driffill from "The Guardian 10/12/17"
Copyright © 2017 by The Guardian Co.

There's more to the Isle of Man than motor racing and tax breaks by Liz Rowlinson from "The Telegraph 03/07/17"
Copyright © 2017 by The Telegraph Co. Reprinted with Permission

Future Predictions For Artifical Intelligence and Automation by Daniel Newman from "Huffpost 30/05/17"
Copyright © by Daniel Newman, Principal Analyst at Futurum Research. Reprinted with Permission

Take more proactive climate action from "The Japan Times 24/11/16"
Copyright © 2016 by The Japan Times Co. Reprinted with Permission

UNESCO "Japanese Food: Intangible Cultural Heritage" by Yukikazu Nagashima from "J–Town Guide Little Tokyo 05/02/14"
Copyright © 2014 by All Japan News Inc. Reprinted with Permission

The Origins of bathhouse culture around the world by Suemedha Sood from "BBC Travel 30/11/12"
Copyright © 2012 by BBC Travel

All 155 Aboard Safe as Crippled Jet Crash-Lands in Hudson By Robert D. McFadden from "The New York Times 16/01/09"
Copyright © 2009 by The New York Times Co. Reprinted with Permission

The history of Hanukkah by Cameron Macphail from "The Telegraph 12/12/17"
Copyright © 2017 by The Telegraph Co. Reprinted with Permission

Fashion History: Dandyism from "College Fashion 20/08/14"
Copyright © 2014 by College Fashion LLC. Reprinted with Permission

A city's art biennial can be like watching an army of curatorial truffle pigs. by Oliver Bennett from "The Guardian 24/02/17"
Copyright © 2017 by The Guardian

Should Literature Be Useful? by Lee Siegel from "The New Yorker 06/11/13"
Copyright © 2013 by The New Yorker Reprinted with Permission

Bottles and bricks still get thrown over the wall... by David Lowe from "The Sun 05/04/16"
Copyright © 2016 by The Sun Co.

On Reading Old Books by William Hazlitt from "The Plain Speaker, 1826"

Marriage by Samuel Johnson from "The Rambler, 19/05/1750"

はしがき

　このテキストは18世紀から2017年までに新聞、雑誌、インターネットに掲載された英文を集め、大学での英語教科書として編まれたものです。ファッション、食文化、テクノロジー、社会、経済、歴史、言語、環境などのジャンルを扱った英文が収録されていますので、学生のみなさんにとって興味深い、あるいは深く考えさせられるようなものが含まれているはずです。対象とする国も、イギリスやアメリカだけでなく、ヨーロッパ各国、アジアなど様々で、これらの英文を読むことで、世界各国の諸相を体感してもらいたいと思っています。

　本書の意図はオーセンティックな英文を読み、読解力を養うと同時に、英文に書かれたことをもとに、自分の意見を発するきっかけを作ることです。易しい英文もあれば、かなり骨の折れる英文もありますが、時代を超えて、読まれ続けるような内容のものを選択しています。英語の資格試験に出題されるようなタイプの英文とは異なりますが、大学生として知的に成長できるよう、収録されている英文に果敢に挑んでみましょう。

　構成としては、まず700〜1400 wordsの英語本文があり、その右欄に注釈と読解を誘導するための小問を付しました。本文の最後には、内容確認のための質問がユニットごとに5問出題され、さらに200字程度の日本語で要約する問題もあります。そして英文に基づき、ディスカッション、またはエッセイ・ライティングのためのテーマも設定されています。問題に沈黙せず、じっくり思考し、自分の考えを発する練習をしてみてください。

　最後に、編集を担当していただいた朝日出版社の朝日英一郎さん、関麻央里さんには大変お世話になりました。この場を借りてお礼申し上げます。

編著者

Contents

Unit: 1		*A 20th-century hero and icon*
Unit: 2		*From Seaspeak to Singlish: celebrating other kinds of English*
Unit: 3		*There's more to the Isle of Man than motor racing and tax breaks*
Unit: 4		*Future Predictions For Artificial Intelligence and Automation*
Unit: 5		*Take more proactive climate action*
Unit: 6		*UNESCO "Japanese Food: Intangible Cultural Heritage"*
Unit: 7		*The Origins of Bathhouse culture around the World*
Unit: 8		*All 155 Aboard Safe as Crippled Jet Crash-Lands in Hudson*
Unit: 9		*The History of Hanukkah*
Unit: 10		*Fashion History: Dandyism*
Unit: 11		*A city's art biennial can be like watching an army of curatorial truffle pigs'*
Unit: 12		*Should Literature Be Useful?*
Unit: 13		*Bottles and bricks still get thrown over the wall …*
Unit: 14		*On Reading Old Books*
Unit: 15		*Marriage*

マンデラの生涯：対立から共生へ	*The Japan Times*, December 10, 2013	3
World Englishesの実例	● *By Rosie Driffill* *The Guardian*, March 11, 2017	8
英・マン島の新たな地域振興策	● *By Liz Rowlinson* *The Telegraph*, July 3, 2017	13
人工知能の未来と人間との関わり	● *By Daniel Newman* *Huffpost*, May 30, 2017	18
気候変動に対する人類の取り組み	*The Japan Times*, November 24, 2016	23
世界に広がる日本の食文化	● *By Yukikazu Nagashima* *J-Town Guide Little Tokyo*, February 5, 2014	28
世界の温浴文化	● *By Suemedha Sood* *BBC Travel*, November 30, 2012	34
ハドソン川の奇跡	● *By Robert D. McFadden* *The New York Times*, January 16, 2009	40
ユダヤ教のハヌカの歴史	● *By Cameron Macphail* *The Telegraph*, December 12, 2017	46
ダンディな生き方とは？	*College Fashion*, August 20, 2014	52
現代美術の祭典ビエンナーレ	● *By Oliver Bennett* *The Guardian*, February 24, 2017	58
文学は有用なのか？	● *By Lee Siegel* *The New Yorker*, November 6, 2013	64
アイルランドに現存する宗派対立	● *By David Lowe* *The Sun*, April 5, 2012	70
読書の愉しみ	● *By William Hazlitt* *The Plain Speaker*, 1826	76
結婚は幸福？	● *By Samuel Johnson* *The Rambler*, May 19, 1750	81

15 Doors to Global Issues

Unit : 1   A 20th-century hero and icon

The Japan Times, December 10, 2013

Today's Topic

昨今のグローバル化に伴い、多種多様な背景や価値観を持つ人々と接触する機会が増えています。同時に、個人間でも国家間でも衝突や紛争が目立つようになっています。我々がこの問題を乗り越えるには何が必要なのでしょうか？ Nelson Mandelaの生涯は、一つのヒントを与えてくれることでしょう。

Nelson Mandela has died. The man who guided South Africa to multiracial democracy, winning the 1993 Nobel Peace Prize in the process, was an icon of the 20th century, a larger-than-life figure who embodied for many the eternal fight for justice.

Mandela's life was a testimony to the need to put aside the anger and desire for vengeance that was rightfully his and to embrace the very best in humanity, regardless of race.

The outline of Mandela's life is well known. He was born July 18, 1918, to the chief councilor to the chief of the Thembu people in Transkei, attended an elite black university but left before completing his studies to join the African National Congress (ANC), and set up its youth wing. He worked as a law clerk and became a lawyer despite the limited opportunities available to blacks in that field. Soon after, Mandela was convicted of violating the Suppression of Communism Act, but his sentence was suspended.

icon「偶像、象徴」

larger-than-life
「誇張された、並外れた」

testimony to ～「～の証明」

embrace「(考えなどを)受け入れる」

Thembu テンブ人（南ア部族の一つ）
Transkei
トランスカイ（南アフリカ共和国にかつて存在した自治区）
African National Congress
「アフリカ民族会議」

Q.1 its は何をさしますか？

(5) While Mandela is today associated with peaceful reconciliation, he was one of the first ANC members to advocate armed resistance to apartheid and was forced underground when he established the armed wing of the ANC. He left South Africa to study the best way to advance the armed struggle and build support for the ANC.

(6) Upon his return to South Africa in 1962, he was arrested and sentenced to five years for incitement and illegally leaving the country. During that incarceration he was charged with sabotage and plotting to overthrow the White government in South Africa.

(7) Called a terrorist by the government that daily terrorized the majority of the South African population, Mandela was sentenced to life imprisonment in 1964 and sent to Robben Island, a penal colony off Cape Town, where he would spend 18 years as one of the world's most famous political prisoners. Several times he was offered a conditional release; in one instance, he would have to renounce violence as a political weapon. He declined, insisting that "What freedom am I being offered while the organization of the people remains banned? Only free men can negotiate. A prisoner cannot enter into contracts."

(8) The effort to isolate and marginalize Mandela was a failure. Ironically it was South Africa that was increasingly marginalized in the world, and Mandela's shadow that grew longer. The majority population of blacks and "colored" in South Africa became increasingly restive, and the thin veneer of

legitimacy that cloaked the apartheid government became ever more shabby. When that government recognized that its time had run out, it turned to Mandela to negotiate a transition to majority rule.

Mandela was released from prison in February 1990, an event that was broadcast live around the world. Talks that were launched while he was in prison became official negotiations between the ANC and the government, culminating in all-race elections in April 1994, a ballot won by the ANC and taking Mandela to the presidency of South Africa, a post he held for one five-year term.

Mandela will be remembered for insisting on the dignity of all humanity, and for refusing, when in prison or in power, to give in to baser instincts. He sought equality and freedom for all South Africans, fighting against white domination and black domination alike. He brought an end to apartheid without sparking a civil war, an outcome many thought inevitable. Not only did Mandela help engineer a peaceful transition, through his efforts he also managed to avoid a mass exodus of the white population as well as the disassembling of the South African economy.

While he was born a leading member of his tribe, Mandela understood the thinking of the people. He appreciated the value of a gesture: His support for the national rugby team, the Springboks, long considered a symbol of white South Africa, won over many Afrikaners. Perhaps his greatest legacy will be the Truth and Reconciliation Commission, which was empowered to grant amnesty for political

---

legitimacy「正当性」
cloak「覆う」
shabby「ぼろぼろの」

Q.2 its は何をさしますか？

culminate in「ついに〜に達する」
ballot「投票」

give in to 〜「〜に屈服する」

engineer「巧みに実行する」
exodus「出エジプト記、多くの人が出て行くこと」

Q.3 a mass exodus とはどういうことですか？

disassemble「ばらばらになる」

gesture「意思表示行為」
Springboks スプリングボクス（ラグビー南アフリカ代表チーム）
win over「人の心をつかむ」
Afrikaner アフリカーナー（南アフリカ共和国の白人）
the Truth and Reconciliation Commission「真実和解委員会」

crimes committed by all sides during the dark years of apartheid if it believed the person seeking amnesty had provided full disclosure.

⑫ South Africa's Truth and Reconciliation Commission is widely considered an outstanding success and a model for similar reconciliation efforts around the world. But essential to its success was the backing of Mandela himself. His unwavering support for justice, rather than revenge, along with his calls for respect and tolerance provided both ballast and guidance for a process that could have easily gone off the rails.

⑬ Of course, there are detractors. For some, an implacable minority, Mandela will always be a communist whose support for liberation movements worldwide—especially those that backed him and his cause when they were outlaws and that Mandela refused to criticize when he was in power—will blacken his image. Some blame him for the failings of subsequent ANC leaders and for the fact that South Africa has failed to realize its potential and is instead mired in political squabbles and corruption.

⑭ South Africa may not be all that it can be, but it is an indication of Mandela's remarkable achievement that his country did not fall apart when he left office. Mandela insisted that "he wanted to be remembered as an ordinary South African who, together with others, has made his humble contribution." Nothing could be further from the truth.

A 20th-century hero and icon Unit : 1

Questions

[A] 本文に基づいて、以下の問いに答えてください。

1. マンデラの生涯は何を証明するものと述べられているか、説明してください。

2. マンデラはアフリカ民族会議で当初どのような活動をしていましたか。

3. マンデラが釈放の申し出を辞退したのはなぜでしょうか。

4. 真実和解委員会とはどのようなものでしょうか。

5. マンデラの偉業は何だと述べられているか、説明してください。

[B] 本文の内容を200字以内の日本語で要約してください。

■ Discussion & Essay Theme

多種多様な背景や価値観を持つ他者と共生してゆくには、何が重要でしょうか？本文の趣旨を踏まえて、自分の意見を論述してください。

Unit : 2
From Seaspeak to Singlish: celebrating other kinds of English

● *By Rosie Driffill*

The Guardian, March 11, 2017

Today's Topic

グローバル化が進むなか、"World Englishes" という概念が注目を浴びています。つまり英語は英語圏のネイティヴ・スピーカーだけのものではなく、世界各国の人々が使用する、お国訛りが入った「英語」をよしとする考え方です。きれいな発音、文法ミスのない完璧な英語の習得を目指している人は、以下の地域の人々が使う英語について考えてみてはどうでしょう？

⑮   It was recently reported that the government is being urged to create opportunities for Britons to learn languages like Polish, Urdu and Punjabi, in order to effect more social cohesion. According
5 to Cambridge professor Wendy Ayres-Bennett, language learning, and indeed social integration, should not be a one-way street; rather, the onus should also fall on British people to learn community languages.

⑯ 10   For me, this idea of a two-way street taps into a wider question about linguistic influence and evolution. There is interest and joy to be had not only in learning the languages of other cultures, but also in appreciating the effect they might have had
15 on English.

⑰   Part of that process is ceding British English to the prospect of change, noting the ways in which ethnically marked forms of English, such as Bangladeshi and African-Caribbean varieties, have
20 played their part in shaping how new generations

Urdu
ウルドゥー語（パキスタンとインドのイスラム教徒の言葉）

Punjabi
パンジャブ語（インド、パキスタンにまたがるエリアの言語）

cohesion「まとまり」

onus「負担」

Q.1 this idea of a two-way street とはどういうことですか？

tap into「〜に入り込む」

cede「譲る」

varieties「異種の言語」

across the country will speak: take Multi-Cultural London English, the dialect that has almost completely replaced Cockney on the streets of the capital.

Outside the UK too, creoles and dialects have bent, broken and downright flipped the bird at the rules, offering not only musicality and freshness, but new ways of conceiving of language that staunch protectionism doesn't allow for. Grammar rules have their place, of course, insofar as they offer a framework for precision and comprehension. But rules can be learned to be broken, leading to the formation of identities, cultural protests and unique means of expression. Not persuaded? Then consider these examples of syntactic rule-bending and linguistic intermarriage that have taken English into intriguing and delightful new directions.

Irish English

Otherwise known as Hiberno-English, this refers to dialects spoken across the island of Ireland. Frank McCourt immortalised West and South-West Irish English in his memoir *Angela's Ashes*, with its liberal use of the definite article ("Do you like the Shakespeare, Frankie?"), and the unbidden musicality that comes with inverted word order ("Is it a millionaire you think I am?").

Some of my friends from Northern Ireland will plump for the past simple form of a verb where a past participle is usually required, saying things like: "They'd never have did it had they knew." Rule breaking at its most ballsy: and it's music to my ears.

Singlish

Short for Colloquial Singaporean English, a creole language for which English is the lexifier (meaning it provides the basis for most of its vocabulary) plus words from Malay, Tamil and varieties of Chinese. The Singaporean government rallies against it at every turn with Speak Good English campaigns, to the detriment of some extremely interesting grammatical structures.

Take Singlish's being topic-prominent, for example: like in Mandarin, this means that Singlish sentences will sometimes start with a topic (or a known reference of the conversation), followed by a comment (or some new information). For example, "I go restaurant wait for you." Grammatically, it's worlds apart from "I'll be waiting for you at the restaurant," but it's evolved in a region where that kind of sentence structure is the order of the day.

Belizean creole (Belize Kriol)

Another English-based creole language, similar to Jamaican patois, which offers some compelling takes on tense. The present tense verb does not indicate number or person, while the past is indicated by putting the tense marker mi in front of the verb ("ai mi ron" – I ran), but this is optional and considered superfluous if a time marker like "yestudeh" (yesterday) is used.

Basic English

Basic English was invented by C.K. Ogden

in 1930. Designed to allow language learners to acquire English quickly and communicate at a very basic level, Ogden managed to reduce the language to 850 words, including only eighteen verbs!

Seaspeak

(25) A controlled natural language(CNL) based on English that provides a lingua franca for sea captains to communicate. First conceived in 1985, the premise is simple, grammar-free phrases that facilitate comprehension in often fraught and dangerous situations. It has now been codified as Standard Marine Communication Phrases.

lingua franca
「(異言語間での)共通語(通商の際使用されるpidgin Englishも含む。)」

premise「前提」

fraught「緊迫した」

codify「成文化する」

(26) Ultimately, English grammar has always been in flux: both in its native land and abroad. When it comes to 'offshoots' of the language, whatever label we apply – be it dialect, patois, creole or CNL – each exists as a yardstick for linguistic evolution, and ought to be celebrated as such.

in flux「流動的で」

offshoot「派生物」

yardstick「基準」

Questions

[A] 本文に基づいて、以下の問いに答えてください。

1. イギリス人の外国語習得についてどのようなことが推察されますか。

2. 現代のロンドンでの英語事情について説明してください。

3. 作家が使ったアイルランド英語の特徴について説明してください。

4. "Singlish"の特徴について記述してください。

5. "creole"の要素をもつ英語は、本章ではどれがあてはまりますか。

[B] 本文の内容を200字以内の日本語で要約してください。

■ Discussion & Essay Theme

英語を外国語として学ぶ日本の教育現場において、どのような英語を学習者に習得させるべきだとあなたは考えますか？本文の事例をもとに、自分の意見を論述してください。

Unit : 3

There's more to the Isle of Man than motor racing and tax breaks

● *By Liz Rowlinson*

The Telegraph, July 3, 2017

Today's Topic

ブリテン島とアイルランド島の間にはマン島（Isle of Man）という島国があります。オートバイ・レースや尻尾のない猫（マンクス）がいることでも有名なこの島は、英王室の属領でありながら、一つの国として機能しています。「タックスヘイブン」としても悪名高いこの地が、いかにして国を盛り立てているのでしょうか？

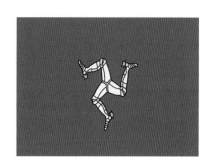

(27) Perhaps it is better known for its TT motorcycle races, when the whole island is suffused with the smell of burning rubber. But the Isle of Man has a rather more historic claim to fame: 600 years ago this week, the Tynwald was founded, which claims to be the oldest continuous parliament in the world. Far from being stuck in the past, this forward-thinking and hi-tech Crown Dependency of just 83,314 people punches far above its weight. Thirty-two years of continuous economic growth, virtually zero unemployment and 10 years of tech infrastructure investment continue to tempt IT workers and e-gaming companies to the British isle.

(28) It was the combined offering of old-fashioned community values and tech sophistication that drew Tom Granger to the Isle of Man from Leicestershire five years ago. The entrepreneur runs a software company and lives with his wife Vicky and two daughters in Port Erin, a popular west coast fishing village with an attractive swathe

---

TT motorcycle
マン島で開催されるバイクレース

suffuse「満たす」

Q.1 the smell of burning rubber とはどういうことですか？

Tynwald
英王室属領であるマン島の立法府

Crown Dependency「英王室属領」

punches above one's weight
「自分の能力よりも勝ると思われることをする」

entrepreneur「起業家」

swathe「帯状の土地」

Victorian
「(19世紀英国) ヴィクトリア朝時代の」

of Victorian seafront villas. "I had visited the island for the TT motor racing event over the years and, because of its good schools, I heard it was ideal for children," says Tom. "We gave it a try for six months and loved it. The girls get to live a freer, safer life than they would on the mainland." Their four-bedroom Victorian townhouse near the beach cost £390,000; the average property price on the island was £265,000 last year. There are plenty of cottages with traditional Manx slate roofs plus a good choice of new-builds; the island's recent Budget included innovative approaches to unlocking development sites for builders.

Those people working in the island's hefty financial services sector, or who want to be close to the airport or King William's College, the international baccalaureate school, gravitate towards the historic capital, says Tim Groves of estate agent Black Grace Cowley. "Demand is strongest around Douglas, especially in the south, focused around Castletown, Port Soderick and Santon," he says. "The buy-to-let market is also strong here, driven by gaming industry employees," who include many of the island's 4,000 South African residents. Gross yields are around five to six per cent.

You can spend £975,000 on a four-bedroom Georgian townhouse, but the lion's share of market activity is between £250,000 to £450,000. "If you head west or north on the island your money goes 30 per cent further," says Neil Taggart of Chrystals estate agency. Both Port Erin and Peel, which has the feel of a mini St Ives, are the west coast hotspots and offer more of a beach holiday feel. There's plenty of room in the north-west of the island for those buyers who want to land their own helicopter on a large, private turnkey property. Near Kirk Michael on the wild west coast, developer Dandara has a new six-bedroom home with a pool, spa and triple-height entrance hall for £5.9 million.

It's more than just the real estate and picturesque locations that lure people to the isle: the attractive tax regime means the top rate is just 20 per cent and there is a cap of £125,000. There is also no stamp duty, inheritance tax or capital gains tax. "We are targeting 25- to 45-year-olds who are making their first million," says Nick Preskey, who provides the government's "concierge service" for high earners moving to the island. There are grants to fledgling businesses too through the government's Enterprise Development Fund. Preskey admits that the island needs 15,000 more people to attract better bars and restaurants. While heather-covered moors and dramatic hills create a bikers' paradise (and produced the cycling "Manx Missile" Mark Cavendish, who is second on the all-time list of Tour de France stage wins), and long sandy beaches wrap around the 100-mile coastline, you'll struggle to find much high-end shopping or dining.

Things are changing, though. The Isle of Man now has artisan gins and a sourdough bread shop, says MaryBeth Coll, a lawyer from Colorado who has recently opened the Foraging Vintners wine bar next to Port Erin's coastguard with her Australian husband, Ian. "The TT and tax were the reasons that brought us here – Ian was working on the rigs until the price of oil fell – so making rhubarb and elderflower wine here was our Plan B," she says. "We just did our first pop-up bar at the TT and had a Glastonbury DJ here for a rave-style party under a pink sunset over our deck."

rig「油田掘削」

rhubarb「ダイオウ（タデ科の多年草）」

elderflower「ニワトコの花」

Q.4 Plan B とはどういうことですか？

rave「レイブ（シンセサイザーによるダンス音楽）」

There's more to the Isle of Man than motor racing and tax breaks　　Unit : 3

Questions

[A] 本文に基づいて、以下の問いに答えてください。

1. マン島の昨今の景気状況について説明してください。

2. マン島へ移住した起業家の事例が紹介されていますが、移住した理由は何ですか。

3. マン島の近年の不動産市場について説明してください。

4. マン島の優遇税制について具体例を挙げてください。

5. マン島産業に新たな領域が加わっています。それについて説明してください。

[B] 本文の内容を200字以内の日本語で要約してください。

■ Discussion & Essay Theme

マン島のような資源のない小国が、観光やタックスヘイブンなどによって地域経済の活性化を図っていることについて、本文の事例をもとに、自分の意見を論述してください。

Unit : 4
Future Predictions For Artificial Intelligence and Automation

● *By Daniel Newman*

Huffpost, May 30, 2017

Today's Topic

人口知能（AI）について近年日本でも多くの報道がなされています。我々の生活に多くの利点をもたらす一方で、現在人間の手で行われている仕事が、人工知能の発達によってそれにとって代わられるのでは、との疑念が数多く出され始めています。果たして近い将来、そういったことが本当に現実化するのでしょうか。

Perhaps the biggest irony about artificial intelligence (AI) is that—despite the many things AI *can* tell us—it can't tell us how it will ultimately impact our lives, economy, or world. In fact, the impact of AI and automation on our job market and economy has been steadily debated—and loudly—for the last few years, with the story constantly changing. With AI advancing at such a fast clip, it's time to get to the bottom of the AI automation issue. Where do we stand? And what outcomes are most likely to shake out in the near term?

Data has shown that AI is already changing several industries. It's also increasing the level of fear among many workers worldwide—for good reason. Studies show almost 40 percent of U.S. jobs are at risk for automation by the early 2030s. There's already a dedicated "human-free zone" at Port Botany in Sydney where shipping cartons are managed by AI robots, rather than people, and it's becoming clear that the impact of AI-managed

at a fast clip 「ものすごい速さで」

shake out 「広がる」

dedicated 「専用の」

carton 「段ボール箱」

jobs extends far further than the work positions themselves. For instance, when automated vehicles threaten the roles of 1.7 million U.S. truck drivers, they won't just be putting those drivers out of work. They will be changing the work of automobile insurance companies … road maintenance crews … highway patrol officers … loading and unloading workers. When AI goes to work, it goes viral.

Still, there is likely no need to bash AI automation for putting the entire nation out of work—yet. The following are a few solid observations about the industry, and how they could impact the new digital workforce.

AI Will Continue to Change Customer Service

Ten years ago, I couldn't go a day without hearing someone complain about the offshoring of customer service. As American companies sought to save money by shipping their call centers overseas, American shoppers threw up their hands, frustrated with communication issues and the sell-off of quality U.S. jobs. Fast forward to 2017, and offshoring is being replaced with chat-shoring—chat bots taking over the customer service routine. In fact, if you've reached out to nearly any company in the past year to settle an overdue bill, clear up an inaccurate charge, or figure out a password issue, you've likely noticed something: it's increasingly difficult to talk to a human. In one of perhaps the only accurately-hyped AI trends, it is estimated that more than 85 percent of customer interactions will be handled by AI by 2020.

(37) Personally, I still wouldn't panic, even if customer service is your industry. Along with AI, customer experience has become a hot-button issue for consumers, and a huge human element needed to accurately address and fulfill human needs will likely remain, at least in the near term.

Human Oversight Is Still Needed

(38) Customer service isn't the only industry where human interaction remains not just a norm, but a necessity. Despite AI's ability to quickly monitor—and even master—huge amounts of data, there are still plenty of glitches with the technology's development. The need for "humans in the loop" will grow alongside AI itself, as humans help validate AI findings, prepare data, and remain vigilant in culling out AI bloopers and mistakes. Until AI can learn from its mistakes and self-correct, a team of humans will be required to find and fix the technology.

Jobs Will be Lost—And Gained

(39) As noted above, it's estimated that one-third of jobs in the US will be automated by the 2030s. That's a hard pill to swallow, especially considering AI has been able to automate everything from driving to writing, performing surgery, diagnosing illness, and everything in between. There is no industry immune from AI's grips. Still, also noted above, the force of AI will be enormous in coming years. As such, humans will likely also create new jobs in the near term to help manage AI and automation.

(40) The truth is, none of us can say at this point

how AI will change the economy or our lives. All we can do is try to remain as agile as possible in our current positions—similar to the way today's businesses need to stay agile to remain competitive or in the black. While some look toward universal basic income as a way to keep humans healthy and housed in the AI storm, I'd say it's a bit too soon to steer so far from civilization's historic course. Humans are needed. Ethics are needed—and they always will be. And the extent of that need will not be decided by AI or automation—it will be decided by all of us.

agile「機敏な」

Q.5 in the black とはどういうことですか？

basic income「最低生活保障（すべての国民に最低限の生活を送るのに必要な額の現金を給付する政策）」

steer「進む」

Q.6 that need とはどういうことですか？

Questions

【A】 本文に基づいて、以下の問いに答えてください。

1. 将来の米国における労働環境についてどのように記述されていますか。

2. カスタマー・サービスセンターの過去と現在について説明してください。

3. 人工知能が発達するなか、どういった状況下で人間が必要とされていますか。

4. 人工知能の発達によってオートメーション化された業界を具体的に挙げてください。

5. 人工知能と人間との関係について、筆者はどのように結論付けていますか。

【B】 本文の内容を200字以内の日本語で要約してください。

■ Discussion & Essay Theme

人工知能は今後われわれの生活のどのような領域において有益なものとなりえるのでしょうか。本文の趣旨に対する賛否を交えて、自分の意見を論述してください。

Unit : 5　*Take more proactive climate action*

The Japan Times, November 24, 2016

Today's Topic

気候変動に対処するために2015年にパリ協定（Paris agreement）が結ばれました。しかしその後のこの協定を巡る世界各国の足並みは必ずしも揃っているわけではありません。2016年のアメリカ大統領選挙でも争点の一つとなりました。日本はどのような役割を果たすことができるのでしょうか？

(41)　Japan lagged behind others in the initial efforts to put the Paris agreement last December into action to combat climate change. Now the nation needs to redouble its work toward the pact's goal of an effectively zero emission of greenhouse gases into the atmosphere by the latter half of the century. Tokyo's failure to ratify the deal before the pact entered into force in early November with the endorsement by dozens of other signatories will be no problem if it can indeed play leading roles in the long and steady international efforts to contain climate change—which need to start today for them to be effective in fighting the manmade rise in global temperatures.

(42)　The first meeting of parties to the Paris accord—held during the COP 22 United Nations conference on climate change in Marrakesh, Morocco—ended by agreeing to draw up by 2018 a rule book to implement steps under the agreement to fight global warming. Japan took part in the

lag behind「遅れる」
Paris agreement「パリ協定」

greenhouse gas「温室効果ガス」

ratify「批准する」

endorsement「承認」
signatory「調印国」

Q.1 it は何をさしますか？

COP 22
「第22回気候変動枠組条約締約国会議」
Marrakesh
マラケシュ（モロッコ中央部の都市）

23

meeting as an observer without voting rights since its ratification of the accord earlier this month was not in time for it to be officially counted as a party to the deal at the gathering. It was after it became certain that the accord will enter into force that the Abe administration submitted a legislation for its ratification to the Diet.

It was significant that the participants in the Marrakesh meeting demonstrated their resolve to move their anti-global warming efforts forward even as the election of Donald Trump, who has described climate change a hoax and pledged to pull the United States out of the agreement, as the next U.S. president cast a shadow over the future of the deal. The U.S. and China—the world's two largest emitters of global warming gases—ratified the Paris accord in September, giving impetus to the procedures by other countries to endorse the pact and put it in force in only 11 months after the deal was struck in December 2015.

The U.S. withdrew from the 1997 Kyoto Protocol against global warming when the then administration of President George W. Bush refused to ratify the treaty. Still, the pact entered into force with the endorsement by other countries, moving forward the international efforts to combat climate change. During the Marrakesh conference, China, the world's top emitter, indicated that it would go ahead with cuts to its own emissions and provide aid to developing economies to help their fight against global warming. What specific policies President Trump will take on the issue remains to be seen, but

Take more proactive climate action **Unit : 5**

the international community including Japan must not let any deviation in the U.S. position on the issue derail worldwide efforts to tackle climate change, and urge the incoming the U.S. administration to stand by the nation's commitment to combat the global problem.

(45)　　Unlike the Kyoto Protocol, the Paris agreement, signed by more than 190 countries last year, requires efforts by both industrialized and developing economies to take on climate change to achieve its goal of keeping the post-Industrial Revolution rise in the world's temperatures within 2 degrees to avert the catastrophic impact of global warming. The problem is, voluntary plans submitted by the participants ahead of the deal are deemed far insufficient to achieve the goal, and the agreement calls on nations to regularly review and beef up their efforts to reduce their emissions.

(46)　　Japan needs to do its own share—and more—of the effort as the world's fifth-largest emitter that accounts for 3.8 percent of global emissions. Environment Minister Koichi Yamamoto said at the Marrakesh gathering that Japan would "play a central role" in the effort to reduce worldwide net emissions to zero through its own emissions cuts as well as financial and technological aid to developing economies. The government's target calls for a 26 percent cut in Japan's emissions in 2030 from the 2013 levels. But the process under the Paris accord for the nations to revamp such goals starts in just a few years. While Abe calls efforts to combat climate change a "top priority" of his Cabinet, there seems

derail「脱線させる」

stand by「(約束などを)守る」

avert「避ける」

beef up「強化する」

Q.4 the world's fifth-largest emitter とは何をさしますか？

net「正味の」

revamp「改訂する」

to be little indication that he spends much of his political resources to deepen Japan's commitments to the fight against global warming.

(47)   Japan's efforts toward cutting its own emissions have failed to impress internationally. While the Marrakesh meeting was being held, environmental think tanks and NGOs reportedly rated Japan's policy on climate change quite poorly, citing its energy policy that relies heavily on supply from coal-fired power plants and its pursuit of nuclear energy as a key alternative to fossil fuels instead of doing more to promote renewable energy. If the government wants to rebut such ratings, it needs to demonstrate that it is serious about combating climate change by taking concrete action and coming up with more ambitious long-term plans.

Take more proactive climate action | **Unit : 5**

Questions

[A] 本文に基づいて、以下の問いに答えてください。

1. 温室効果ガスに関するパリ協定の目標を説明してください。

2. パリ協定の第一回会合において、日本が投票権のない傍聴国として参加したにすぎなかった理由を説明してください。

3. パリ協定に対するアメリカと中国の姿勢をそれぞれ説明してください。

4. 気温上昇に関するパリ協定の数値目標を説明してください。

5. 気候変動に対する日本の政策が国際的に評価されていないのはなぜでしょうか。

[B] 本文の内容を200字以内の日本語で要約してください。

■ Discussion & Essay Theme

地球温暖化に対処するに当たって、日本はどのような役割を果たすことができると考えられますか？本文の趣旨に対する賛否を交えて、自分の意見を論述してください。

Unit : 6
UNESCO "Japanese Food : Intangible Cultural Heritage"

● *By Yukikazu Nagashima*

J-Town Guide Little Tokyo, February 5, 2014

Today's Topic

昨今、日本の文化が多くの国の人々を引きつけています。その一つが和食です。これを目当てに日本を訪れる観光客も少なくありません。のみならず、和食を提供する店は世界各地に広がっています。和食は2013年に無形文化遺産に登録されました。和食はどのようにして世界に知られるようになり、人気を博すようになったのでしょうか？

(48) UNESCO (The United Nations Educational, Scientific and Cultural Organization) decided to register "*Washoku*" (traditional Japanese cuisine) as an Intangible Cultural Heritage on December 4, 2013 during the intergovernmental panel at Azerbaijan, Baku. That was recommended by the Japanese government. Until now Gastronomy Art of France, Mediterranean Cuisine, Traditional dishes of Mexico, and Traditional kashkak of Turkey have been registered as Intangible Cultural Heritage, but the food culture of the country as a whole having been recognized as Intangible Cultural Heritage are only France and Japan. "*Washoku*" is the fifth culinary Intangible Cultural Heritage registered by UNESCO.

(49) The Japanese government proposed the registry of *Washoku* to UNESCO last March, citing "various fresh fruits from the mountains and seas due to geographic diversity," "presentation that capitalizes on the beauty of nature," "close relationship between

---

UNESCO
「国際連合教育科学文化機関」

Intangible Cultural Heritage
「無形文化遺産」

panel「委員会」

Baku
バクー（アゼルバイジャンの首都）

gastronomy「美食」

cuisine「料理（法）」

kashkak
ケシケキ（麦や肉、ミルクなどを煮込んで作るトルコの料理）

culinary「料理の」

capitalize on ～
「～を利用する」

the New Year and rice planting," and other highly cultural aspects of Japanese cuisine. UNESCO's subsidiary agency that conducted the preliminary review in October had recommended the "registry"
25 of *Washoku* as "playing an important role in social solidarity."

(50) The Intangible Cultural Heritage is one of UNESCO's Heritage Project Programs, along with "World Heritage" and "Memory of the World."
30 *Washoku* constitutes the twenty-second registry from Japan following kabuki and Noh, etc. Because *Washoku* has already become widespread in the U.S. followed by Europe, it's entirely possible that the cuisine's global popularity was a sufficient factor
35 that led to the decision to register Japanese cuisine as an Intangible Cultural Heritage. The logic is, if the popularity of *Washoku* were limited domestically within Japan, then the decision to register Japanese cuisine as an Intangible Cultural Heritage would
40 have never occurred. From this perspective, the contributions by trading corporations that spread the popularity of *Washoku* are huge. We spoke to Noritoshi Kanai, Chairman of the Mutual Trading Company, one of such major trading companies in
45 the world.

The challenge to make sushi widespread

(51) The Mutual Trading Company is located south of Little Tokyo. Founded in 1926, the Mutual Trading
50 started exporting Japanese food products to the U.S. in full-scale in 1951, the year that then-President Chuhei Ishii asked current Chairman Kanai to join

the company.

(52) During World War II, Kanai was sent to the front lines in Burma. In Burma, approximately 300,000 Japanese soldiers died, of which 95 percent was due to the fact that the food did not reach the front lines. After the war, Kanai became involved in the business of distributing Japanese food to Japanese people living in the U.S. A lesson he learned during the war was a factor in his career choice.

(53) At the beginning, Mutual Trading achieved a big success by importing and selling Japanese cookies. Those were made in a special way of baking. But major U.S. makers started making similar cookies and the Mutual Trading was unable to compete with those major companies.

(54) The Mutual Trading Company eventually decided to only handle Japanese products, as recommended by Harry Wolff Jr., a former Jewish food broker, which led to their decision to sell sushi in the United States. At the time, very few people in the U.S. knew of sushi in the mid-'60s.

(55) Deciding between supermarkets and restaurants to make sushi widespread, Kanai chose to focus on restaurants. He proposed starting a sushi bar to make sushi more accessible to local diners. Kanai paid frequent visits to major Japanese restaurant "Kawafuku" in Little Tokyo at the time to recommend installing a sushi bar. Six months later, "Kawafuku" finally agreed, offering the first sushi bar in the U.S. The term "sushi bar" was also Kanai's idea.

(56) The following year, "Eigiku" in Little Tokyo

followed suit, followed by "Tokyo Kaikan" also installing a sushi bar a year after "Eigiku." American diners gradually started to enjoy sushi. Once sushi became widespread in the U.S., its popularity started to spread like "flying sparks" from Little Tokyo to Japanese restaurants in other regions. Caucasian sushi chefs started to emerge, and sushi gradually spread to West Los Angeles regions.

Food related products become widespread

Of course preparing sushi requires rice. Not any rice, but rice that's most suitable for making sushi rice. In this way, business with the Koda Farm that produces suitable rice for sushi in California started, followed by expanded importation of soy sauce, vinegar, seaweed, and other food products needed to prepare sushi. Freezing food for preservation became widespread in the mid-'60s, a method that offers vast improvement over ice placed in bags to transport fish by air.

Also, importation of sake that accompanies sushi also became widespread, along with cooking utensils. Sashimi knives, professional cutting boards, soy sauce dispensers and dishes, etc., expanded Mutual Trading's inventory of products.

On the other hand, the supply of sushi chefs was also an issue. The demand for sushi chefs in the U.S. greatly expanded from late 1960s to the '70s, which brought many sushi chefs from Japan. At the time, VISAs were easily obtainable legally. However, once non-Japanese sushi professionals started to emerge, obtaining VISAs became gradually difficult.

⑥⓪ On the other hand, the inflated Yen due to the second oil shock decreased the value of U.S. dollars in the U.S., which decreased the number of sushi chefs coming to the U.S. This trend continued, which led to Kanai's decision to form a partnership with an established sushi restaurant to jointly start a sushi-chef school in 2008, which has produced approximately a hundred sushi chefs to date.

⑥① Due to this flow of events, Kanai states, "Japanese cuisine received a lot of criticism when it was first introduced to the world. It became widespread because the cuisine itself is appealing. We were fortunate to be able to help it become widespread."

⑥② "The only countries in the world to have their cuisine recognized as an Intangible Cultural Heritage are only France and Japan. This is a great accomplishment. By having our cuisine recognized as an Intangible Cultural Heritage, jobs relating to Japan's culinary cuisine will continue to expand," said Kanai, as he drew from an important lesson on distribution he learned from his wartime experiences.

---

inflate「(価格を)上昇させる」

the second oil shock
第二次石油ショック

Q.6 This trend とはどのようなものですか?

UNESCO "Japanese Food : Intangible Cultural Heritage"　　Unit : 6

Questions

[A] 本文に基づいて、以下の問いに答えてください。

1. 日本政府はユネスコに和食の登録を申請する際、和食の特徴をどのようにアピールしたのでしょうか。

2. 和食が無形文化遺産に登録される上で、貿易会社はどのような点で貢献したと言えるのでしょうか。

3. 金井紀年が日本食の貿易に携わる要因となった戦時中の教訓とはどのようなものでしょうか。

4. 金井は寿司をどのようにアメリカに広めたのか、説明してください。

5. 金井によると、和食の無形文化遺産への登録によって今後何が期待されるでしょうか。

[B] 本文の内容を200字以内の日本語で要約してください。

■ Discussion & Essay Theme

一国の食文化を世界に広めることにはどのような意義があると考えられますか？本文に述べられている事例を参考に、自分の意見を論述してください。

Unit : 7
The Origins of bathhouse culture around the world

● *By Suemedha Sood*

BBC Travel, November 30, 2012

Today's Topic

日本は現在、温泉ブームと言っていいかもしれません。「おんせん県」と自県の名前を付けて観光をアピールしているところもあるぐらいですから。世界に目を向けてみると、日本の温泉に似た施設がたくさんあることに気づかされます。トルコ、韓国、フィンランドの事例をみて、各国の温浴文化について考えてみましょう。

(63) Hot baths, saunas, steam rooms, hot springs – spa culture takes on various forms throughout the world, and learning to relax like a local is a top attraction in many destinations. But as entwined as
5 bathhouse culture has become with many modern day societies, the seemingly omnipresent practice of using heat to release toxins is actually tens of thousands of years old, dating back to the Neolithic Age when nomadic tribes would find relief from
10 the bitter cold by soaking in the various natural hot springs they stumbled upon around the world.

(64) One of the world's earliest known public baths was built in the Indus Valley around 2500 BC in the lost city of Mohenjo-daro. Called the "Great
15 Bath", this large pool constructed of baked brick was excavated in the early 1900s by archaeologists in present-day Pakistan. Anthropologists say it may have been used as a temple, since bathing and cleanliness may have been linked to religious beliefs.

(65) 20 Much later, around 300 BC, the practice of

entwine「絡ませる」

toxin「毒」

Neolithic Age「新石器時代」

nomadic「遊牧の」

Q.1 they は何をさしますか？

stumble upon「思いがけず見つける」

Mohenjo-daro
インダス文明最大級の都市遺跡

excavate「発掘する」

anthropologist「人類学者」

public bathing was adopted by the Romans, and the bath became a vital part of society, visited by rich and poor. For many it was the only place to rinse off after a long week of manual labour and at the time, crowds of men and women bathed naked together, as the bath was a primary place to gather and socialize. The tradition of the public bath has since spread around the world, adapting to evolving cultures and social norms with differing customs and etiquette for each destination.

Turkish hammam

Turkish baths, called hammams, were likely derived in part from Roman and Byzantine baths – an export of the Roman Empire that extended to Turkey in the 7th Century. The concept was predicated on having places of extreme cleanliness, where purifying the body went hand-in-hand with purifying the soul. Popularized around 600 AD, hammams were also spaces where major life events were celebrated, and bathing rituals were incorporated into weddings and births.

The hammam is still a common gathering place for socializing and relaxing today. Upon entering, visitors may be given a towel, a pair of sandals and an abrasive mitt, a *keşe* – meant for exfoliating the skin. The hammam typically consists of three main areas: a hot steam room with a large marble stone at the centre, where bathers lay as attendants scrub them and administer massages; a warm room for bathing; and a cool room for resting. Areas are typically gender-separated and nudity is optional.

One historic hammam worth visiting is Istanbul's Cagaloglu Hamami, a palatial marble bathhouse that was built in 1741.

Japanese onsen

(68) Japanese onsen are natural hot springs, born from the country's plentiful volcanic activity, and the practice of soaking in these thermal baths for healing, spirituality and rejuvenation stems back to when Buddhism spread to Japan in the 500s. Some evidence suggests that Buddhist monks had a hand in founding some of the earliest spa-like spots around the country.

(69) Since Japan's onsen are based around natural formations, some have been around for thousands of years. One such place is Dogo Onsen, located on the island of Shikoku, believed to have been in use for at least 3,000 years. Mentions of the onsen have been found in texts from early Japanese history, illustrating it as the great leveller, welcoming gods, emperors and peasants alike. There is a certain cultural protocol to keep in mind when visiting a Japanese hot spring resort (nudity is required, for example).

Korean jimjilbang

(70) Disrobing is also mandatory in jimjilbangs, or Korean bathhouses, which are always separated by gender. Jimjilbangs are a family affair in South Korea, with everyone from children to the elderly joining in on the pastime. The origins of this tradition could be linked to the country's natural

hot springs, some of which have been in use for more than a thousand years. Today, many jimjilbangs are open 24-hours and offer lodging for the night, perfect for weary travellers. Also unique to Korea are the materials used in the saunas, steam rooms and hot tubs. For instance, jade may be used in the sauna to relieve joint pain and stress, while baked clay may be used to promote detoxification. Body scrubs are also very common, using a mitt similar to the Turkish keşe, but with milk and water to moisturize the skin while promoting circulation.

(71)   One of the more famous jimjilbangs in Seoul is the massive Dragon Hill Spa, a seven-storey spa featuring a seawater bath, a salt room, saunas, baths, a swimming pool, a fitness centre, gardens, a food court, a nail salon, a golf course, an internet cafe and a movie theatre. The primary draw is the main sauna, heated by charcoal and infused with an oak aroma.

Finnish sauna

(72)   Saunas are ubiquitous in Finland, a country with around two million saunas, or approximately one sauna for every two or three people. Nearly all Finns "take a sauna" at least once a week and many families own portable saunas to take on camping trips. "Sauna" is even a Finnish word, meaning a hot steam bath – the steam for which is created by pouring water over heated stones.

(73)   Although the origins of the Finnish sauna are murky, Finland's cold climate likely contributed to the creation of this heat-filled structure. According

to the documentary "Steam of Life", a film focused on Finland's spa obsession, some of the first saunas were heated huts that also served as homes. In addition to bathing, saunas would have been used for chores requiring high heat, such as curing meats, and practices requiring sterile environments, such as preparing to bury the dead.

(74) The traditional Finnish sauna – which dates back to at least the 12th Century – is a smoke sauna, heated by a wood stove with no chimney. After soaking in the heat, many locals will head outside to roll around in the snow or jump into a hole in a frozen-over lake, since going from hot to cold is thought to stimulate blood circulation. The oldest public sauna still in use in Finland is the Rajaportin Sauna, a smoke sauna dating back to 1906 and located in the southern city of Tampere. To stay in Finland and not take a sauna would be like visiting Ancient Rome and not stopping at the local bathhouse. What better place to experience this age-old tradition than a historic spa that helped shape the customs of today?

The Origins of bathhouse culture around the world | **Unit : 7**

Questions

【A】 本文に基づいて、以下の問いに答えてください。

1. 世界で最も初期の温浴施設について説明してください。

2. 現在のトルコでみられる温浴施設のシステムと設備について説明してください。

3. 日本の温泉と仏教との関わりについて説明してください。

4. 「サウナ」とは何語で、元々どういう意味をもつ単語ですか。

5. 温浴施設に入る際、裸になることが求められるのはどの文化圏でのことですか。

【B】 本文の内容を200字以内の日本語で要約してください。

■Discussion & Essay Theme

本文で扱った国々の温浴施設のうち、どこの国のものが魅力的だと感じましたか？日本の温泉との違いについても考慮しながら、自分の意見を論述してください。

Unit : 8

All 155 Aboard Safe as Crippled Jet Crash-Lands in Hudson

● *By Robert D. McFadden*

The New York Times, January 16, 2009

Today's Topic

2009年1月15日、乗員乗客155名を乗せてニューヨークを出発したUSエアウェイズの旅客機は、離陸直後にエンジンが停止する未曾有の事態に見舞われました。この時、機長が下した判断は・・・。この出来事は2016年に映画化され話題となりました。あわやの大惨事はどのようにして回避されたのでしょうか？

(75)   A US Airways jetliner with 155 people aboard lost power in both engines, possibly from striking birds, after taking off from La Guardia Airport on Thursday afternoon. The pilot ditched in the icy
5 Hudson River and all on board were rescued by a flotilla of converging ferries and emergency boats, the authorities said.

(76)   What might have been a catastrophe in New York—one that evoked the feel if not the scale of
10 the Sept. 11 attack—was averted by a pilot's quick thinking and deft maneuvers, and by the nearness of rescue boats, a combination that witnesses and officials called miraculous.

(77)   As stunned witnesses watched from high-rise
15 buildings on both banks, the Airbus A320, which had risen to 3,200 feet over the Bronx and banked left, came downriver, its fuselage lower than many apartment terraces and windows, in a carefully executed touchdown shortly after 3:30 p.m. that
20 sent up huge plumes of water at midstream, between

jetliner「ジェット旅客機」

La Guardia Airport ラガーディア空港（ニューヨーク市にある国際空港）

ditch「水上に不時着する」

flotilla「船隊」

converge「群がる」

avert「避ける」

deft「巧みな」

maneuver「操作」

Q.1 a combination とは具体的に何と何の組み合わせですか？

Bronx ニューヨーク市の5つの区の一つ

fuselage「機体」

plume「（空中にたちのぼる煙や水などの）柱」

West 48th Street in Manhattan and Weehawken, N.J.

(78)　On board, the pilot, Chesley B. Sullenberger III, 57, unable to get back to La Guardia, had made a command decision to avoid densely populated areas and try for the Hudson, and had warned the 150 passengers to brace for a hard landing. Most had their heads down as the jetliner slammed into the water, nose slightly up, just three minutes after takeoff on what was to be a flight to Charlotte, N.C.

(79)　Many on board and watching from the shores were shocked that the aircraft did not sink immediately. Instead, it floated, twisting and drifting south in strong currents, as three New York Waterway commuter ferries moved in. Moments later, terrified passengers began swarming out the emergency exits into brutally cold air and onto the submerged wings of the bobbing jetliner, which began taking in water.

(80)　As the first ferry nudged up alongside, witnesses said, some passengers were able to leap onto the decks. Others were helped aboard by ferry crews. Soon, a small armada of police boats, fireboats, tugboats and Coast Guard craft converged on the scene.

(81)　Over the next hour, as a captivated city watched continuous television reports and the Hudson turned from gold to silver in the gathering winter twilight, all of the passengers, including at least one baby, and both pilots and all three flight attendants, were transferred to the rescue boats—a feat that unfolded as the white-and-blue jetliner continued to drift south.

⑧² When all were out, the pilot walked up and down the aisle twice to make sure the plane was empty, officials said. Brought ashore on both sides of the river, the survivors were taken to hospitals in Manhattan and New Jersey, mostly for treatment of exposure to the brutal cold: 18 degrees in the air, about 35 degrees in the water that many had stood in on the wings up to their waists.

⑧³ Still, most of them walked ashore, some grim with fright and shivering with cold, wrapped in borrowed coats. But others were smiling, and a few were ready to give interviews to mobs of reporters and television cameras. Some described their survival as a miracle, a sentiment repeated later by city and state officials; others gave harrowing accounts of an ordeal whose outcome few might have imagined in such a crisis.

⑧⁴ Even the aircraft was saved for examination by investigators—towed down the Hudson and tied up at Battery Park City. In the glare of floodlights, the top of its fuselage, part of a wing and the blue-and-red tail fin jutted out of the water, but its US Airways logo and many of its windows were submerged.

⑧⁵ "We've had a miracle on 34the Street," Gov. David A. Paterson said at a late-afternoon news conference in Manhattan. "I believe now we've had a miracle on the Hudson. This pilot, somehow, without any engines, was somehow able to land this plane, and perhaps without any injuries to the passengers. This is a potential tragedy that may have become one of the most magnificent days in the history of New York City agencies." Mayor Michael R. Bloomberg said that there had been few injuries and that the pilot had done "a masterful job."

The National Transportation Safety Board and state and local agencies are to investigate the cause of the crash, which could take months, but early indications were that the plane's engines had shut down after having ingested a flock of birds—variously described as geese or gulls. It was not clear where the birds were encountered.

The pilot radioed air traffic controllers on Long Island that his plane had sustained a "double bird strike." Without power, returning to the airport was out of the question, aviation experts said. He saw a small airport in the distance, apparently at Teterboro, N.J., but decided to head down the Hudson and make a water landing, a rare event that is mentioned in the safety instructions given by flight crews to all passengers on every flight.

Aviation experts said such a maneuver is tricky. An angle of descent that is too steep could break off the wings and send the aircraft to the bottom. Witnesses in high-rise buildings on both sides of the river described a gradual descent that appeared to be carefully controlled, almost as if the choppy surface of the Hudson were a paved tarmac.

Susan Obel, a retiree who lives on West 70th Street and Amsterdam Avenue in a 20th-floor apartment, saw the plane flying amazingly low. "When you see a plane somewhere that it isn't supposed to be, you get that eerie feeling," she said. "I didn't think it was a terrorist, but I did worry."

⑨⁰　　On the plane, passengers heard the pilot say on the intercom, "Brace for impact." One passenger, Elizabeth McHugh, 64, of Charlotte, seated on the aisle near the rear, said flight attendants shouted more instructions: feet flat on the floor, heads down, cover your heads. "I prayed and prayed and prayed," she said. "Believe me, I prayed."

⑨¹　　Tom Fox, president of New York Water Taxi, which sent boats to the scene in the Hudson but did not participate in the rescues, said the setting was, in a sense, ideal for a crash landing on water. "It couldn't have gone down in a better location," he said. "The pilot must have been both talented and charmed."

flat
「(床・壁などに) ぴったり身をつけて」

charmed「強運の」

All 155 Aboard Safe as Crippled Jet Crash-Lands in Hudson Unit : 8

Questions

[A] 本文に基づいて、以下の問いに答えてください。

1. 大惨事が回避された要因は何と述べられているか、二点挙げてください。

2. 空港に引き返せないと判断した機長は何をすることを決断しましたか。

3. 乗客全員が機外に出た後、機長は機内で何をしましたか。

4. ニューヨーク州知事がこの出来事を「奇跡」と呼んだのはなぜでしょうか。

5. この事故の原因は何と述べられているか、説明してください。

[B] 本文の内容を200字以内の日本語で要約してください。

■ Discussion & Essay Theme

思いがけない出来事に遭遇した際、それに対処する上で重要なことは何だと考えられますか？本文の事例や指摘を参考に、自分の意見を論述してください。

Unit : 9 The history of Hanukkah

● *By Cameron Macphail*

The Telegraph, December 12, 2017

Today's Topic

キリスト教圏では12月になると、クリスマス関連行事が至るところで開催されます。日本でもそれは同じです。一方で、このクリスマスとほぼ同じ頃に、ユダヤ教を信じる人々は、この宗教独自の儀礼的なお祭りを祝う習慣があります。「ハヌカ」(Hanukkah)と呼ばれるそのイベントはどのようなものなのでしょうか。

Hanukkah, the eight-day Jewish festival also known as the Festival of Lights, see Jews around the world light one candle on a nine-branched menorah – or 'hanukiah candelabrum' – each day. The holiday begins on the 25th day of Kislev, which is the ninth month of the ecclesiastical year on the Hebrew calendar. In the western calendar, Hanukkah is celebrated in November or December. This year it begins Tuesday 12 December and continues until Wednesday 20 December.

What is the history behind Hanukkah?

The word Hanukkah means 'rededication' and commemorates the Jews' struggle for religious freedom, when the leaders of a Jewish rebel army called the Maccabees rose up against their Greek-Syrian oppressors in the Maccabean Revolt of 167 BC (BCE). King Antiochus had taken over the Second Temple in Jerusalem and soon after ordered an altar to Zeus to be erected. Judaism was prohibited,

menorah　メノラ（燭台）

hanukiah candelabrum「ハヌカの燭台」

Kislev　ユダヤ暦の9月

ecclesiastical「教会の」

rededication「再献納」

Maccabees
「マカバイ家（ユダヤの指導者の一族）」

King Antiochus
アンティオコス4世（プトレマイオス朝を倒し、後にマカバイ戦争を起こす。）

Second Temple
バビロニアによって破壊されたものに代わって出来た神殿で、ユダヤ教礼拝の中心地。

altar「祭壇」

Judaism「ユダヤ教」

circumcision was banned and pigs were ordered to be sacrificed at the altar. The Jewish rebellion that followed was led by Judah Maccabee, (or Y'hudhah HaMakabi, meaning "Judah the Hammer"). The uprising spanned three years until the Maccabees gained control of Jerusalem.

Judaism's central text the Talmud, dictates only pure olive oil with the seal of the high priest can be used for the Hanukiah. They wanted to rededicate the desecrated temple, but could find only one container of the sacred oil needed which had the seal of the high priest still intact. The candelabrum is required to burn throughout the night every night but, according to legend, although there was only enough oil for one day the candles miraculously stayed alight for eight days – the time needed to prepare a fresh supply of kosher oil for the menorah. This event became known as 'the miracle of the oil' and is now marked with this eight-day festival.

And what about traditional Hanukkah food?

For Hanukkah, Jews customarily eat fried foods to commemorate the miracle associated with the temple oil. 'Sufganiyot' are round deep-fried jam or custard-filled doughnuts which are topped with powdered sugar. These are said to derive from a yeast dough pastry mentioned in the Talmud. These pastries were cooked in oil and called sufganin (absorbent) because they absorbed a lot of oil in cooking. In more Northern communities, where olive oil was scarce and expensive, goose or chicken fat was often used for frying so potato pancakes (latkes), apple fritters, and other non-dairy fried foods became the norm.

Why are dairy products popular during Hanukkah?

During the Babylonian captivity of the Jews, the town of Bethulia in Judea was under siege and its population on the verge of surrender due to lack of water. A young woman called Judith requested a meeting with Nebuchadnezzar's top General, the Assyrian Holofernes, who was directing the siege outside the town walls. She entered the Holefernes camp and seduced him, fed him salty cheeses so that he would become thirsty and served him wine so he would fall asleep. She then killed him and returned to the town with his severed head. The Assyrians, having lost their leader, fled and Israel was saved. Judith remained unmarried for the rest of her life and in memory of her bravery and purity Jews make sure to eat dairy products during Hanukkah. Nowadays, even though olive oil is affordable, dairy is often added on top of a latke – usually in the form of a dollop of sour cream.

Is it Chanukah or Hanukkah?

In Hebrew, Hanukkah is pronounced with the letter 'chet'. The letter "H" makes the closest sound, so both names work and can be used.

Celebrating Hanukkah with a dreidel

Games are often played during the festival, including spinning the dreidel which is the Yiddish word for a spinning top. A dreidel is a pointed, four-sided top which can be made to spin on its pointed base. Dreidels are normally made of plastic or wood and there is a Hebrew letter embossed or printed on each of the dreidel's four sides. These four letters form the acronym of the phrase: "Nes gadol hayah sham," "A great miracle happened there"; a reference to the Hanukkah miracle of the oil. The dreidel dates back to the time of the Greek-Syrian rule over the Holy Land – the one which set off the Maccabean revolt (see above). Learning Torah was outlawed by the enemy, a 'crime' punishable by death and Jewish children were forced to study in secret. If the Greeks came calling, the pupils would pull out their tops and pretend to be playing a game.

Hanukkah in popular culture

Jewish comedian Adam Sandler was a regular on *Saturday Night Live* before he became famous for starring in terrible movies. In 1994 Sandler wrote and performed 'The Chanukah Song', a novelty ditty which deals with the issue of Jewish children feeling alienated during the Christmas season. Sandler lists Jewish celebrities (both real and fictional) as a way of sympathising with the children's situation. Many fans of popular culture previously unfamiliar with the festival first became aware of Hanukkah after an episode of the popular sitcom *Friends* aired in December 2000. Ross, who is entertaining his young (and half-Jewish) son Ben during the week of Christmas, tries at the last minute to find a Santa costume. The only outfit available is an armadillo so he creates a new holiday character called 'The

Holiday Armadillo' – Santa's south-of-the-border friend who teaches Ben about the importance and history of Hanukkah.

Questions

[A] 本文に基づいて、以下の問いに答えてください。

1. ハヌカはいつ行われますか。

2. ハヌカの際、伝統的にどういったものが食べられますか。

3. ハヌカと乳製品との関わりについて説明してください。

4. 「ドライデル」とはどういう形態のものか、記述してください。

5. ハヌカが認知されたきっかけを、大衆文化との関連で説明してください。

[B] 本文の内容を200字以内の日本語で要約してください。

Discussion & Essay Theme

キリスト教の宗教的儀式であるクリスマスを祝う時期に、ユダヤ教の宗教的儀式であるハヌカも祝われます。異なる宗教が共存することの意義について、自分の意見を論述してください。

Unit : 10 Fashion History: Dandyism

College Fashion, August 20, 2014

Today's Topic

我々にとってファッションとは何なのでしょうか。それは単に服装に関するものではなく、我々の生き方に関わるものかもしれません。ファッションの用語として広く知られているダンディ(Dandy)の歴史を題材に、ファッションについて考えてみてはどうでしょうか？

The author of the poem "Candy is dandy but liquor is quicker" got it all wrong: any self-respecting dandy would agree that liquor trumps candy when it comes to "dandiness." So does sartorial elegance, quick-witted banter, and quoting "The Flowers of Evil", probably.

But the elusive images of exclusive gentlemen clubs, smoky salons, and top hats hide, or at least disguise, the true definition of a dandy. Let us then embark on the noble quest of defining, identifying, and maybe seeking out the modern version of such a rare breed. Who were or even are dandies? On whose side are they?

The Birth of a Myth

Finding out the origins of the heroes of our quest requires a brief time travel to London in the late 18th century. If we're careful to avoid the horse carriages, we may be lucky enough to make Sir Beau Brummell's acquaintance, and he will tell us

---

"Candy is dandy but liquor is quicker"
アメリカの詩人オグデン・ナッシュの詩

trump「〜に勝る」

sartorial「紳士服の」

quick-witted「機転が利く」

banter「軽口」

"The Flowers of Evil"
フランスの詩人ボードレールの詩集

elusive「捉えどころのない」

top hat「シルクハット」

Q.1 such a rare breed とは何のことですか？

a rare breed
「めったにいないタイプの人」

horse carriage「馬車」

Sir Beau Brummell
洒落者ブランメル（ジョージ・ブライアン・ブランメルの異名）

everything he knows about the topic while smoking a cigar in his decorous apartment, probably.

⑬ Dandies, he'll sure say, never come from upper classes. Those in the ups, lords and such, think their lifestyle ordinary and, so, pay little attention to the lavish beauty of art or exquisite mastery of their cooks. They need someone from the middle class, an intelligent loner, to show them the pleasures of a beautiful life.

⑭ Dandies appeared at the crossroads of the end of aristocracy and the birth of democracy. They came to define the "new" aristocracy: reminiscent of the English ideas about the perfect gentleman, yet with no blue blood to back it up. Dandyism is a cult of a person, not background. If you're more amusing than the prince, who cares if your father is merely a politician, am I right? (Brummell is smirking, probably.)

The Dandy Evolution

"Dandyism is the aesthetic form of nihilism."
—Jean Baudrillard

⑮ After Beau hints that it is time for you to leave (as it is time for his boots to be polished with champagne), don't ask amateur questions: a proper dandy is always an eccentric myth. They could be guest lecturers in any Public Relations class. Dandyism is a flirtatious relationship with the public: the right amount of societal scandal or juicy rumors keep the passion alive.

⑯ Oscar Wilde gave actress Lillie Langtry a lily every day—as a play on her name—and didn't get offended at the papers for calling him foolish. He knew the *Gossip Girl* motto before it was the *Gossip Girl* motto: you're no one until you're talked about.

(17) We're leaving Brummell's apartment to pay a visit to 19th century Paris, where the "second wave" of dandyism occurred, and invited Baudelaire to be our guide. Closer to bohemian ideas, Parisian dandies made beauty and art, rather than manners into a cult. Vulgarity was the enemy and simplicity the ultimate sophistication. The Baudelairian dandy is too narcissistic to ever fall in love with another person. He's too busy reading Byron or turning his life into art.

(18) The third and final stage of dandyism is commercial, marketable. While the original dandies valued emotional reserve and calmness, the likes of Oscar Wilde found beauty in the artificial and the exaggerated—a suffocating perfume or flamboyant colors.

(19) Susan Sontag describes this as a phenomenon called "Camp:" a show of coded messages for the "knowing" crowd and carnival masks that have on/off modes. This ironic stage of dandyism then dissipated into the sweet monstrousness of decadence.

On Gender and Fashion

(20) Dandies were obsessed with "the other." Everything French was considered most fashionable in England and, of course, vice versa. Mr. Wilde called his infamous infatuation with Lord Alfred a consequence of his love for paradoxes applied to the world of emotions. The paradoxes of gender have

---

Q.3 it は何をさしますか？

Baudelaire ボードレール
bohemian「ボヘミアン」（自由奔放な生活をする人）

vulgarity「下品」

narcissistic「自己陶酔的な」
Byron イギリスの詩人

suffocate「息苦しくさせる」
flamboyant「派手な」

Susan Sontag アメリカの作家

dissipate「消散する」
decadence「退廃」

infatuation「のぼせあがり」
Lord Alfred イギリスの作家、詩人、翻訳家

always been an essential part of dandyism.

(21)   A man spending five hours daily on his appearance seems feminine, while dandy women have always preferred masculine clothes. "The most womanly woman," (according to Musset), George Sand, dressed in drag to go on fashionable (at the time) strolls around Paris without attracting unwanted attention.

(22)   Coco Chanel, the dandiest woman of the fashion world (according, well, to me), was inspired by traditional English gentlemen costumes and the dandyism principle of "conspicuous inconspicuousness." She advised her clients to "dress like their maids" and changed the meaning of black from mourning to chic. Chanel was also the first one to accidentally set a trend. After a geyser explosion, she had to cut her slightly-burnt hair short. Like a true dandy, she valued an air of carelessness and comfort in fashion.

(23)   Oscar Wilde, too, took part in fashion revolutions. In contrast to Coco, he liked purple, gold, and ornamental details, but the general principle of "functional chic" still stands: he actively supported Dress Reform, an 1880 women's movement against corsets and high heels.

(24)   Throughout history dandies have pioneered many fashion trends and movements—changing tastes from impeccable simplicity to much-discussed eccentricity and back again—but their fashion has always been just another aspect of the personality cult.

Spot the Dandy

(25)   So, where is (s)he, the modern dandy? Maybe what's left is a Halloween costume idea, an anachronism, a dream, a joke? Maybe we can find only pieces of the image, or read fashionable novels to recreate the pseudo-good old days of dandy clubs and narcissistic romance.

(26)   Or, could it be that dandies are all around us? Those who wear ideas pulled right from the runways or their imaginations, who turn their whole life into a piece of art in an Instagram-mosaic of only the dandiest pieces.

(27)   The emotional walls and self-admiration in selfies, the cult of beauty, the cult of vulgarity, exaggeration, masks, Camps, gender benders, and more personal blogs than people on the planet. Dandyism is in full swing. Yet no one is the audience.

Fashion History: Dandyism **Unit : 10**

Questions

[A] 本文に基づいて、以下の問いに答えてください。

1. Dandyismが生まれたのはいつ頃で、何を崇拝するものかを説明してください。

2. "you're no one until you're talked about." (p.54, l.55)とはDandyismどのような面を表す言葉でしょうか。

3. Dandyismの「第二の波」とはどのようなものでしょうか。

4. Coco Chanelが「ダンディ」と評されるのはなぜでしょうか。

5. 今や"Dandyism is in full swing." (p.56, l.133)と言われる根拠は何か、説明してください。

[B] 本文の内容を200字以内の日本語で要約してください。

■ Discussion & Essay Theme

Dandyismのどのような面が現代の我々の生き方に当てはまり、その功罪はどのように考えられますか？本文の趣旨に対する賛否を交えて、自分の意見を論述してください。

Unit : 11
A city's art biennial can be like watching an army of curatorial truffle pigs

● By Oliver Bennett

The Guardian, February 24, 2017

Today's Topic

美術鑑賞といえば、これまで美術館などの建物内で鑑賞することが一般的でした。しかしながらこの数十年で、現代美術の展示法に新たな形態が加わりました。ビエンナーレやトリエンナーレという単語を耳にしたことはないでしょうか。これらは隔年（3年ごと）に都市や地域が会場となって現代美術を屋外（内）展示し、地域振興をマッチングさせたイベントなのです。

It was like a cultural version of Davos, held in the wintry grandeur of central Oslo. For three days, delegates and guests sat in a conference called Oslo Pilot, holding critical discussions about "relational aesthetics" and the role of public art in society. But really, last November's event was all about one question: should the Norwegian capital climb aboard the crowded urban bandwagon and host an art biennial?

Oslo is expecting 30% population growth and two major museum re-launches over the next few years. As one of the curators of Oslo Pilot, Per Gunnar Eeg-Tverbakk, says: "Oslo is already rich in culture, with two sculpture parks in a city of just over 600,000." In which case, what's the point of having a biennial? "There's been an explosion of biennials, triennials and their ilk, and so many cities now have one," observes Charles Esche, director of Eindhoven's Van Abbemuseum.

Normally a temporary but recurrent exhibition,

Davos
世界経済フォーラムが開催されるスイス東部にあるリゾート地

delegate「代表団」

bandwagon「流行」

biennial「隔年行事（ビエンナーレ）」

triennial
「三年に一回開催される行事（トリエンナーレ）」

ilk「同類」

Van Abbemuseum
（オランダにある）ファン・アッベ美術館

recurrent「再発する」

the every-two-year form is the most prevalent – whether for reasons of practicality or historical precedent. And they are indeed blossoming: from Beijing to Berlin, Taipei to Sao Paulo. So legion are these exhibitions that it's hard to quantify how many cities now have them, although rough estimates put the total at between 200 to 300 – up from single figures in the 1960s and 70s.

(31) And while biennials have traditionally focused on contemporary art, an increasing number are breaking into sectors such as design and architecture – the connecting idea being that they are a showcase of the cerebral, the avant garde, the bleeding edge. "A biennial puts your city on the map and it's great city marketing," says Rafal Niemojewski of the Biennial Foundation. Biennials represent a mobilisation of art and visitors; they're a feel-good moment for cities to connect to a wider network. "People in remote cities can see international, contemporary art without having to travel to New York or Paris," says Niemojewski. "That sense of cultural traffic is a huge incentive."

(32) Esche dates the biennial boom to the late 1980s: "When the cold war ended, cities across the world started to compete with each other," he says. This model lives on in the boosterish boilerplate of contemporary biennials: the Toronto biennial, mooted to start this year, is trumpeting "Toronto's arrival on the international stage as a global visual arts powerhouse".

(33) Esche says biennials are often driven by local politicians seeking to "circulate symbolic capital"

for intangible future gain; and that they're a "quicker fix" than an "iconic" new museum, with none of the aggravation. "City councils tend to love them," says Christian Oxenius of the Institute of Cultural Capital. "Biennials have become a kind of 'brand' in themselves, and they indicate membership of a wider club."

Also, biennials are unregulated – anyone can host one. There's no Olympic Committee or Fifa equivalent; and bar a couple of observational bodies such as the four-year-old International Biennial Association, there's no corporate oversight at all. But perhaps that's their strength.

The locust effect

The first biennial is still the most famous: Venice, born 1895. When it was started by then mayor, Riccardo Selvatico, the Venice biennale hoped to ride the growing move in bourgeois cultural tourism. "Venice was a promotional tool for the city," says Esche. "And that aspect has stayed."

While cultural tourism remains a goal to this day, biennials gradually became freighted with other ideas, including political positioning. "In the 1950s, a few biennials emerged which widened reasons for staging them," Oxenius says. "For example, in 1951 the Sao Paulo biennial [said to be the second oldest in the world] was founded when Brazil was forming a modern national cultural identity." Four years later, Alexandria in Egypt hosted the Biennial of the Mediterranean as a post-colonial message.

As biennials are often seeking a breakthrough

in global awareness for their host cities, Niemojewski points out that they often tend to be held in more peripheral cities: "It's notable that London, Madrid and Paris don't have biennials but Lyons, Seville and Liverpool do."

Oxenius suggests another key reason why they're attractive: "Biennials are relatively cheap – far cheaper than a big sporting event." And because they are temporary they can bypass planning – yet claim to be a catalyst for change: creating cultural infrastructure just as the Olympics aims to motivate sports in local populations. Istanbul, which started in 1987 (when it was only the sixth biennial in the world) became a "tool to explain the city anew", according to Esche. When he worked on Istanbul biennial in 2005, he says it was an opportunity to re-conceptualise Istanbul as a contemporary, cosmopolitan city, rather than the backwards-gazing tourist narrative of Ottoman grandeur.

At best, art biennials can positively transform our engagement with cities. But there are perceived disadvantages to this phenomenon. They have, for example, been seen as a precursor of gentrification, and there's also the suggestions that biennials drive a kind of top end, transnational tourism – as if they are a moving playpen for the 10,000 globe-flitting critics, collectors and curators that constitute the international art world.

At worst, biennials are dominated by VIP sections and can become part of a global search for art as a luxury asset – an attitude that sits particularly ill at ease in poorer cities. "In some contexts they raise a host of complexities," says James Brett of The Museum of Everything gallery. Esche has also identified a "locust effect", whereby biennials come in and eat up a city's cultural resources. "Then those local big wigs who wanted it in the first place say, 'We've now done contemporary art' – and it all stops, leaving no money for other cultural projects."

Yet Oxenius believe the biennial model has plenty of life left in it – provided these events work hard to be inclusive, and to engender a sense of place. "My feeling is that biennials can help transform our perceptions of cities, and play an important role in the development of communities," he says. So will launching a biennial make people think differently about Oslo? "There are so many hundreds of biennials asking more or less the same things, using more or less the same model," concedes co-curator Eva González-Sancho, who is hopeful the Norwegian capital will get its new biennial within the next couple of years. "So we will do something different."

A city's art biennial can be like watching an army of curatorial truffle pigs | **Unit : 11**

Questions

[A] 本文に基づいて、以下の問いに答えてください。

1. "That sense of cultural traffic"（p.59, l.41）とはどういうことですか、説明してください。

2. ビエンナーレ・ブームが起こったのはいつ、どのような時期ですか。

3. 最初に行われたビエンナーレについて説明してください。

4. ビエンナーレが流行している理由を複数挙げてください。

5. ビエンナーレのマイナス面を挙げてください。

[B] 本文の内容を200字以内の日本語で要約してください。

■ Discussion & Essay Theme

ビエンナーレやトリエンナーレが世界各国をはじめ、日本でも多く開催されるなか、芸術が地域振興に利用されているとの否定的な見方も存在します。本文の趣旨に対する賛否を交えて、自分の意見を論述してください。

Unit : 12 Should Literature Be Useful?

● By Lee Siegel

The New Yorker, November 6, 2013

Today's Topic

昨今の教育現場では、実用的な文章読解がカリキュラムに入れられ、小説や詩などの文学作品を読む機会が減りつつあります。そのようななかで、非実用的なものとしてみられがちな「文学」に対する新たな見解が提示されました。文学は有益だとの学術的な実験結果が出たのです。果たして純文学作品のもたらす効用とはどのようなものなのでしょうか？

(42)   Two recent studies have concluded that serious literary fiction makes people more empathetic, and humanists everywhere are clinking glasses in celebration. But I wonder whether this is a victory
5 for humanism's impalpable enrichments and enchantments, or for the quantifying power of social science.

(43)   The two studies divided participants into several groups. The methodology was roughly the same in
10 both studies. One group read selected examples of literary fiction; another read commercial fiction, and another was given serious non-fiction or nothing at all. The subjects were asked either to describe their emotional states, or instructed, among other tests,
15 to look at photographs of people's eyes and try to derive from these pictures what the people were feeling when the photographs were taken.

(44)   The results were heartening to every person who has ever found herself, throughout her freshman
20 year of college, passionately quoting to anyone

---

literary fiction「文芸小説」
empathetic「共感できる」
(< empathy「感情移入」)
clink glasses「祝杯をあげる」

Q.1 this とは は何をさしますか？

impalpable「非常に理解しがたい」
quantify「定量化する」

commercial fiction「大衆小説」

subject「被験者」

derive「得る」

hearten「勇気づける」

within earshot Kafka's remark that great literature is "an axe to break the frozen sea inside us." The subjects who had read literary fiction either reported heightened emotional intelligence or demonstrated that their empathy levels had soared beyond their popular- and non-fiction-reading counterparts.

The studies' conclusions are also particularly gratifying in light of the new Common Core Standards, hastily being adopted by school districts throughout the country, which emphasize non-fiction, even stressing the reading of train and bus schedules over imaginative literature. Here at last, it seemed, was a proper debunking of that skewed approach to teaching the art of reading.

There is another way to look at the studies' conclusions, however. Instead of proclaiming the superiority of fiction to the practical skills allegedly conferred by reading non-fiction, the studies implied that practical effects are an indispensable standard by which to judge the virtues of fiction. Reading fiction is good, according to the studies, because it makes you a more effective social agent. Which is pretty much what being able to read a train schedule does for you, too.

Americans have always felt uncomfortable about any cultural activity that does not lead to concrete results. "He that wastes idly a groat's worth of his time per day, one day with another, wastes the privilege of using one hundred pounds each day": though Benjamin Franklin was fairly indifferent to money himself, the sentiment he expressed in that bit of advice became a hallmark of the national character. Idleness is still anathema in American life. And the active daydream of writing and reading fiction is idleness in its purest state, neither promising nor leading to any practical or concrete result. From the didactic McGuffey Readers that lasted from the middle of the nineteenth century to the middle of the twentieth century to William Bennett's "Book of Virtues" in our own time, the American impulse to make room for literature by harnessing it to a socially useful purpose has taken many forms.

Perhaps it is appropriate, in our moment of ardent quantifying—page views, neurobiological aperçus, the mining of personal data, the mysteries of monetization and algorithms—that fiction, too, should find its justification by providing a measurably useful social quality such as empathy. Yet while the McGuffey Readers and their descendants used literature to try to inculcate young people with religious and civic morality, the claim that literary fiction strengthens empathy is a whole different kettle of fish.

Though empathy has become something like the celebrity trait of emotional intelligence, it doesn't necessarily have anything to do with the sensitivity and gentleness popularly attributed to it. Some of the most empathetic people you will ever meet are businesspeople and lawyers. They can grasp another person's feelings in an instant, act on them, and clinch a deal or win a trial. The result may well leave the person on the other side feeling anguished or defeated. Conversely, we have all known bookish, introverted people who are not good at puzzling out

⁸⁵ other people, or, if they are, lack the ability to act on what they have grasped about the other person.

⁽⁵⁰⁾ To enter a wholly different realm, empathy characterizes certain sadists. Discerning the most refined degrees of discomfort and pain in another ⁹⁰ person is the fulcrum of the sadist's pleasure. The empathetic gift can lead to generosity, charity, and self-sacrifice. It can also enable someone to manipulate another person with great subtlety and finesse.

⁽⁵¹⁾ ⁹⁵ Literature may well have taught me about the complex nature of empathy. There is, for example, no more empathetic character in the novel or on the stage than Iago, who is able to detect the slightest fluctuation in Othello's emotional state. Othello, ¹⁰⁰ on the other hand, is a noble and magnanimous creature who is absolutely devoid of the gift of being able to apprehend another's emotional states. If he were half as empathetic as Iago, he would be able to recognize the jealousy that is consuming his ¹⁰⁵ treacherous lieutenant. The entire play is an object lesson in the emotional equipment required to vanquish other people, or to protect yourself from other people's machinations. But no one—and no study—can say for sure whether the play produces ¹¹⁰ more sympathetic people, or more Iagos.

⁽⁵²⁾ Indeed, what neither of the two studies did was to measure whether the empathetic responses led to sympathetic feeling. Empathetic identification with the ordeals suffered by Shakespeare's King Lear, ¹¹⁵ Dostoevsky's Raskolnikov, or Emma Bovary— empathetic sharing of these characters' emotions could well turn a person inward, away from humanity altogether. Yet even if empathy were always the benign, beneficent, socially productive trait it is celebrated as, the argument that producing empathy is literature's cardinal virtue is a narrowing of literary art, not an exciting new expansion of it.

Fiction's lack of practical usefulness is what gives it its special freedom. When Auden wrote that "poetry makes nothing happen," he wasn't complaining; he was exulting. Fiction might make people more empathetic—though I'm willing to bet that the people who respond most intensely to fiction possess a higher degree of empathy to begin with. But what it does best is to do nothing particular or specialized or easily formulable at all.

It's safe to say that, like life itself, fiction's properties are countless and unquantifiable. If art is made ex nihilo—out of nothing—then reading is done in nihilo, or into nothing. Fiction unfolds through your imagination in interconnected layers of meaning that lift the heavy weight of unyielding facts from your shoulders. It speaks its own private language of endless nuance and inflection. A tale is a reassuringly mortalized, if you will, piece of the oceanic infinity out of which we came, and back into which we will go. That is freedom, and that is joy—and then it is back to the quotidian challenge, to the daily grind, and to the necessity of attaching a specific meaning to what people are thinking and feeling, and to the urgency of trying, for the sake of love or money, to profit from it.

Should Literature Be Useful? **Unit : 12**

Questions

[A] 本文に基づいて、以下の問いに答えてください。

1. 実験において各グループの被験者が読まされたものを具体的に挙げてください。

2. "the new Common Core Standards" (p.65, ll.28-29) とはどのようなものですか。

3. 文学の良さを理解することと "practical effects" (p.65, l.39) との関係性を説明してください。

4. アメリカ人の文化的行為に対する特質を具体的に書いてください。

5. イアーゴーはどのような例として挙げられているのか、説明してください。

[B] 本文の内容を200字以内の日本語で要約してください。

■ Discussion & Essay Theme

文学が役に立つとすれば、どういう点でそのように言えるのでしょうか？本文の趣旨に対する賛否を交えて、自分の意見を論述してください。

Unit : 13

Bottles and bricks still get thrown over the wall...

● By David Lowe

The Sun, April 5, 2012

Today's Topic

イデオロギー対立の象徴であったベルリンの壁が壊されてから四半世紀以上が経過しました。しかしながら、英領北アイルランドの首府ベルファストには、プロテスタント系居住区とカトリック系居住区を分断する壁が存在し、21世紀の今も宗派対立が残存していることを我々に示してくれます。この地の人々を隔てる「壁」の現状について考えてみましょう。

Clutching marker pens, some of the young visitors scrawl messages of peace in the gaps between the psychedelic graffiti brightening the otherwise grim barrier. This isn't Germany, where tourists and artists flocked to leave their mark on the Berlin Wall before it was pulled down in 1989. It is a so-called "Peace Wall" in Belfast. There are 99 of these structures in the city and they were built to keep apart communities of Catholics and Protestants.

Today is the 14th anniversary of the 1998 Good Friday Agreement, which promised a new beginning for troubled Northern Ireland. But with widespread support for the peace walls among Catholics and Protestants, they won't be torn down any time soon. In an attempt to change this, a £2million initiative was launched in January aimed at improving community relations and eventually removing the blights on the landscape.

At 875 yards long, the structure on Cupar Way, West Belfast, is among the largest in the city and

clutch「握る」

scrawl「殴り書きする」

psychedelic「幻覚状態を想起させるような」

graffiti「落書き」

grim「不快な」

Berlin Wall 冷戦下のイデオロギー対立を象徴する独・ベルリンにあった壁

Good Friday Agreement 北アイルランド紛争を終息させた和平協定

tear down「壊す」

Q.1 this は何をさしますか？

blight「障害」

it has earned a place on the tourist trail. But for those who live in its shadow, the Cupar Way wall is no visitor attraction. Few tourists signing the Cupar Way peace wall realise how close it comes to the two-up two-down houses in Bombay Street on the other side. During widespread rioting in 1969, the cul-de-sac was burned to the ground by Loyalists.

Now rebuilt, the Catholic residents even have cages over their gardens to stop missiles thrown over the wall injuring them or damaging their property. Among them is Mary Mooney, 43, who has been here since 1998 and watched the divide slowly grow over the years to its current height. From the front upstairs bedroom of her home she can see through the 45ft peace wall wire to the rooftops of the Protestant neighbourhood beyond. As the crow flies it's about 300ft away, but to walk there around the wall would take ten minutes. Mary says: "I wouldn't like the barrier to come down, no way. I'm not comfortable with that because we still get debris thrown over. If there's a Rangers and Celtic match and the Rangers lose then there'll be bottles, bricks, whatever they can get their hands on."

Accompanying today's youth group on a tour is English teacher Stephane Trahard, from Reims, France, who is here for the third time. Stephane, 44, says: "On my first visit I was surprised people in Belfast like to keep the walls. In Berlin the first thing they wanted to do was tear the wall down. It is interesting because although the conflict in Northern Ireland is over, the communities have not healed." A colourful city sightseeing bus roars past, with a group of Japanese snapping photos. Further up the road a couple of black cabs pull over to let their foreign passengers get a closer look at the wall.

(60) So-called "Troubles Tourism" has proved a valuable source of income for firms such as Paddy Campbell's Black Cab Tours, which ferries tourists round notorious locations. One driver, who gives his name as Des, says: "The conventional taxi game is over and this provides me with a living. Everyone who comes to Belfast wants to see the bits that don't get put on the ads."

(61) Another guide, Eamonn McGuckin, says: "Today I have a group from the Netherlands. They are amazed to see walls like these dividing a European city in 2012. I explain that for people living in this area the walls are a way of life. Yes, it would be nice to see them taken down, but people here would not allow it. It's too risky — they fear what could happen."

(62) Shockingly, two thirds of deaths in Belfast related to the Troubles between 1966 and 2003 occurred within 500 yards of a peace wall. One of the most bizarre barriers runs up the middle of Alexandra Park in North Belfast. It's a pretty place with a duck pond, play area and hilly woodland. Only the ugly 9ft wall and the odd scorched tree trunk hint at the park's history. Ironically, the divide was first put up here on September 1, 1994 — the day after the IRA declared its first ceasefire. Protestant and Catholic youths at either end of the green space were waging war for ownership, so a simple fence was put up to separate them. Over the

years it became a permanent, reinforced corrugated steel structure, essentially making two parks out of one.

(63) Last September there was a small step forward when a gate opened in the middle of the barrier, allowing pedestrians to access both sides between 9am and 3pm. Today an elderly lady called Phyllis and a friend have strolled to the gate shortly before it is due to close. They live at opposite ends of Alexandra Park. Phyllis says: "I grew up here and it used to be for everybody. It didn't matter what you were. I think the wall is awful. What kind of a place is this, where even the parks have to be divided?" Just after 3pm a Belfast City Council van pulls up and two workers jump out. They heave the gate shut with a bang and lock it. Alexandra Park is divided once more.

(64) Dr Adrian Johnston is chairman of the International Fund For Ireland, an independent organisation promoting reconciliation in Northern Ireland. The scheme will work with residents to promote the tearing down of barriers. Dr Johnston says: "In 2008 a survey found four out of five people wanted the walls removed when the time is right. The initiative will move at the pace the communities want it to, but there is already an interest. There is a desire to change."

(65) Local charity The Belfast Interface Project is also working with the city's divided communities to speed up the removal of peace walls. Strategic director Joe O'Donnell believes there are three main reasons why they remain despite the peace process

set in motion with the Good Friday Agreement. Joe says: "Fear, safety and security are the things people need to have resolved before the removal of walls becomes possible. These blockades were put up in consultation with residents of the areas at the time. That is how they will be removed. After 30 years of the Troubles the walls won't disappear overnight. They are, after all, a physical representation of the barriers in people's heads."

blockade「障害物」

Bottles and bricks still get thrown over the wall... **Unit : 13**

Questions

[A] 本文に基づいて、以下の問いに答えてください。

1. "Peace wall"とはどのようなものなのか、説明してください。

2. "Peace wall"そばに住むカトリック信徒の女性の周辺環境について記述してください。

3. "Troubles Tourism" (p.72, l.56)とはどういうものですか。

4. Alexandra Parkにある"gate"はどのようなものなのか、説明してください。

5. "Peace wall"の撤去について住人はどのように考えていますか。

[B] 本文の内容を200字以内の日本語で要約してください。

■ Discussion & Essay Theme

21世紀の現在、キリスト教の宗派対立がイギリスに存在する現状についてあなたはどう思いますか？本文の趣旨に対する賛否を交えて、自分の意見を論述してください。

Unit : 14   On Reading Old Books

● By William Hazlitt

The Plain Speaker, 1826

Today's Topic

昨今、様々な形態の書籍が溢れる一方で読書離れも指摘されています。我々にとって読書とはどのような意義を持つものなのでしょうか？鋭い鑑識眼を持つ批評家であると同時にエッセイの名手としても名を馳せたウィリアム・ハズリットは、自身の体験を交えて読書について熱く語っています。これをきっかけに、読書について今一度考えてみてはどうでしょうか。

I HATE to read new books. There are twenty or thirty volumes that I have read over and over again, and these are the only ones that I have any desire ever to read at all. It was a long time before I could bring myself to sit down to the *Tales of My Landlord*, but now that author's works have made a considerable addition to my scanty library. I am told that some of Lady Morgan's are good, and have been recommended to look into *Anastasius*; but I have not yet ventured upon that task. A lady, the other day, could not refrain from expressing her surprise to a friend, who said he had been reading *Delphine*:—she asked,—If it had not been published some time back? Women judge of books as they do of fashions or complexions, which are admired only 'in their newest gloss.' That is not my way. I do not think altogether the worse of a book for having survived the author a generation or two. I have more confidence in the dead than the living. Contemporary writers may generally be divided

Tales of My Landlord
サー・ウォルター・スコットによる1816年から数回に渡って出版された小説

Lady Morgan
レディ・モーガン・シドニー（アイルランド生まれの小説家）

Anastasius
『アナスタシウス』（トーマス・ホープによる1819年の小説）

Delphine
『デルフィーヌ』（スタール夫人による1802年の小説）

gloss「つや」

into two classes—one's friends or one's foes. Of the first we are compelled to think too well, and of the last we are disposed to think too ill, to receive much genuine pleasure from the perusal, or to judge fairly of the merits of either. One candidate for literary fame, who happens to be of our acquaintance, writes finely, and like a man of genius; but unfortunately has a foolish face, which spoils a delicate passage:—another inspires us with the highest respect for his personal talents and character, but does not quite come up to our expectations in print. All these contradictions and petty details interrupt the calm current of our reflections. If you want to know what any of the authors were who lived before our time, and are still objects of anxious inquiry, you have only to look into their works. But the dust and smoke and noise of modern literature have nothing in common with the pure, silent air of immortality.

When I take up a work that I have read before (the oftener the better) I know what I have to expect. The satisfaction is not lessened by being anticipated. When the entertainment is altogether new, I sit down to it as I should to a strange dish,—turn and pick out a bit here and there, and am in doubt what to think of the composition. There is a want of confidence and security to second appetite. New-fangled books are also like made-dishes in this respect, that they are generally little else than hashes and *rifaccimentos* of what has been served up entire and in a more natural state at other times. Besides, in thus turning to a well-known author, there is not only an assurance that my time will not be thrown away, or my palate nauseated with the most insipid or vilest trash, but I shake hands with, and look an old, tried, and valued friend in the face, compare notes, and chat the hours away. It is true, we form dear friendships with such ideal guests—dearer and more lasting than those with our most intimate acquaintance. In reading a book which is an old favourite with me (say the first novel I ever read) I not only have the pleasure of imagination and of a critical relish of the work, but the pleasures of memory added to it. It recalls the same feelings and associations which I had in first reading it, and which I can never have again in any other way. Standard productions of this kind are links in the chain of our conscious being. They bind together the different scattered divisions of our personal identity. They are landmarks and guides in our journey through life. They are pegs and loops on which we can hang up, or from which we can take down, at pleasure, the wardrobe of a moral imagination, the relics of our best affections, the tokens and records of our happiest hours. They are 'for thoughts and for remembrance!'

A sage philosopher, who was not a very wise man, said, that he should like very well to be young again, if he could take his experience along with him. This ingenious person did not seem to be aware, by the gravity of his remark, that the great advantage of being young is to be without this weight of experience, which he would fain place upon the shoulders of youth, and which never comes too late with years. Oh! what a privilege to be able to let this hump, like Christian's burthen, drop from off one's back, and transport one's self, by the help of a little musty duodecimo, to the time when 'ignorance was bliss!' For myself, not only are the old ideas of the contents of the work brought back to my mind in all their vividness, but the old associations of the faces and persons of those I then knew, as they were in their life-time—the place where I sat to read the volume, the day when I got it, the feeling of the air, the fields, the sky—return, and all my early impressions with them. This is better to me—those places, those times, those persons, and those feelings that come across me as I retrace the story and devour the page, are to me better far than the wet sheets of the last new novel from the Ballantyne press, to say nothing of the Minerva press in Leadenhall-street. It is like visiting the scenes of early youth.

musty「かびくさい、古くさい」
duodecimo「十二折判」
ignorance is bliss
「無知は幸福」
（トマス・グレイの詩の一節）

retrace「辿り直す」
devour「むさぼる」
Ballantyne
バランタイン（スコットランドの印刷業者）
Minerva press
ウィリアム・レーンによってロンドンにあるLeadenhall Streetに設立された出版社

Questions

[A] 本文に基づいて、以下の問いに答えてください。

1. どのような本の選び方が "my way" (p.76, ll.16-17) ではないのでしょうか。

2. 現存する著作家よりもすでに世を去った著作家の方が信頼するに足るのはなぜでしょうか。

3. 馴染みの著作家を再読する際には、新しい本を読む際に生じるどのような心配がないのでしょうか。

4. "links in the chain" (p.78, l.66) とはどのようなことを表す比喩か、説明してください。

5. 再読が我々に与えてくれる「特権」とはどのようなものでしょうか。

[B] 本文の内容を200字以内の日本語で要約してください。

■Discussion & Essay Theme

我々にとって読書の意義とはどのようなものと考えられますか？本文の趣旨に対する賛否を交えて、自分の意見を論述してください。

Unit : 15　*Marriage*

● *By Samuel Johnson*
The Rambler, May 19, 1750

Today's Topic

昨今、結婚に対する考え方が多様化しています。その根底にあるのは、結婚は人生に幸福をもたらすのかどうか、という問題でしょう。18世紀の文人サミュエル・ジョンソンは結婚について機知とユーモアに富むエッセイを残しています。これを機に、この問題について考えてみるのはどうでしょうか？

(69)　There is no observation more frequently made by such as employ themselves in surveying the conduct of mankind, than that marriage, though the dictate of nature, and the institution of providence,
5 is yet very often the cause of misery, and that those who enter into that state can seldom forebear to express their repentance, and their envy of those whom either chance or caution has withheld from it.

(70)　This general unhappiness has given occasion
10 to many sage maxims among the serious, and smart remarks among the gay; the moralist and the writer of epigrams have equally shown their abilities upon it; some have lamented, and some have ridiculed it; but as the faculty of writing has been chiefly a
15 masculine endowment, the reproach of making the world miserable has been always thrown upon the women, and the grave and the merry have equally thought themselves at liberty to conclude either with declamatory complaints, or satirical censures,
20 of female folly or fickleness, ambition or cruelty,

employ oneself in ~ing 「~することに専念する」
dictate 「命令」
institution 「制定」
providence 「摂理」
forebear 「慎む」
repentance 「後悔」

sage 「賢明な」
maxim 「格言」

epigram 「警句」

endowment 「資質」

grave 「まじめな」

declamatory 「演説調の」
folly 「愚行」
fickleness 「移り気、浮気」

extravagance or lust.

(71)   Led by such a number of examples, and incited by my share in the common interest, I sometimes venture to consider this universal grievance, having endeavoured to divest my heart of all partiality, and place myself as a kind of neutral being between the sexes, whose clamours, being equally vented on both sides with all the vehemence of distress, all the apparent confidence of justice, and all the indignation of injured virtue, seem entitled to equal regard. The men have, indeed, by their superiority of writing, been able to collect the evidence of many ages, and raise prejudices in their favour by the venerable testimonies of philosophers, historians and poets; but the pleas of the ladies appeal to passions of more forcible operation than the reverence of antiquity. If they have not so great names on their side, they have stronger arguments; it is to little purpose that Socrates, or Euripides, are produced against the sighs of softness, and the tears of beauty.

(72)   But I, who have long studied the severest and most abstracted philosophy, have now, in the cool maturity of life, arrived to such command over my passions, that I can hear the vociferations of either sex without catching any of the fire from those that utter them. For I have found, by long experience, that a man will sometimes rage at his wife, when in reality his mistress has offended him; and a lady complain of the cruelty of her husband, when she has no other enemy than bad cards. I do not suffer myself to be any longer imposed upon by oaths on one side, or fits on the other; nor when the husband

hastens to the tavern, and the lady retires to her closet, am I always confident that they are driven by their miseries; since I have sometimes reason to believe, that they purpose not so much to soothe their sorrows, as to animate their fury. But how little credit soever may be given to particular accusations, the general accumulation of the charge shows, with too much evidence, that married persons are not very often advanced in felicity; and, therefore, it may be proper to examine at what avenues so many evils have made their way into the world. With this purpose, I have reviewed the lives of my friends, who have been least successful in connubial contracts, and attentively considered by what motives they were incited to marry, and by what principles they regulated their choice.

One of the first of my acquaintances that resolved to quit the unsettled thoughtless condition of a bachelor, was Prudentius, a man of slow parts, but not without knowledge or judgment in things which he had leisure to consider gradually before he determined them. Whenever we met at a tavern, it was his province to settle the scheme of our entertainment, contract with the cook, and inform us when we had called for wine to the sum originally proposed. This grave considerer found by deep meditation that a man was no loser by marrying early, even though he contented himself with a less fortune; for estimating the exact worth of annuities, he found that, considering the constant diminution of the value of life, with the probable fall of the interest of money, it was not worse to have ten thousand pounds at the age of two and twenty years, than a much larger fortune at thirty; for many opportunities, says he, occur of improving money, which if a man misses, he may not afterwards recover.

Full of these reflections, he threw his eyes about him, not in search of beauty, or elegance, dignity, or understanding, but of a woman with ten thousand pounds. Such a woman, in a wealthy part of the kingdom, it was not very difficult to find; and by artful management with her father, whose ambition was to make his daughter a gentlewoman, my friend got her, as he boasted to us in confidence two days after his marriage.

Thus, at once delighted with the superiority of his parts, and the augmentation of his fortune, he carried Furia to his own house, in which he never afterwards enjoyed one hour of happiness. For Furia was a wretch of mean intellects, violent passions, a strong voice, and low education, without any sense of happiness but that which consisted in eating, and counting money. Furia was a scold. They agreed in the desire of wealth, but with this difference, that Prudentius was for growing rich by gain, Furia by parsimony. Prudentius would venture his money with chances very much in his favour; but Furia very wisely observing that what they had was, while they had it, *their own*, thought all traffic too great a hazard, and was for putting it out at low interest, upon good security. Prudentius ventured, however, to insure a ship, at a very unreasonable price, but happening to lose his money, was so tormented with

augmentation「増加」

wretch「哀れな人」

Q.3 but の用法を説明してください。
scold「口やかましい人」

parsimony「極度の倹約」

Q.4 it は何をさしますか？
traffic「取引」
put out「投資する」
security「担保」
insure「保険を引き受ける」

the clamours of his wife, that he never durst try a second experiment. He has now grovelled seven and forty years under Furia's direction, who never once mentioned him, since his bad luck, by any other name than that of "the insurer."

durst　dareの過去形

grovel「腹這う、屈服する」

insurer「保険業者、保険屋」

Questions

【A】 本文に基づいて、以下の問いに答えてください。

1. 結婚が "This general unhappiness" (p.81, l.9) と表現されるのはなぜでしょうか。

2. この文章で著者が結婚した友人の人生について述べる目的は何でしょうか。

3. Prudentiusが結婚を考えた理由は何でしょうか。

4. FuriaとPrudentiusの財産に対する考え方の違いを説明してください。

5. FuriaがPrudentiusを "the insurer" (p.85, l.121) と呼ぶようになったのはなぜでしょうか。

【B】 本文の内容を200字以内の日本語で要約してください。

■ Discussion & Essay Theme

結婚が幸福なものとなるには何が重要と考えられますか？本文の指摘や例を参考に、自分の意見を論述してください。

世界を読み解く15の扉

検印 省略	© 2019 年 1 月 31 日　初 版 発 行 2023 年 1 月 31 日　第 3 刷 発 行

編著者　　　　　　　河　原　真　也

　　　　　　　　　　伊　藤　健一郎

発行者　　　　　　　原　　雅　久

発行所　　　　株式会社　朝 日 出 版 社

　　　　101-0065　東京都千代田区西神田 3-3-5
　　　　　　　　　電話　東京　03-3239-0271
　　　　　　　　　FAX　東京　03-3239-0479
　　　　　　　　　e-mail　text-e@asahipress.com
　　　　　　　　　振替口座　00140-2-46008
　　　　　　　組版／ease　製版／錦明印刷

本書の一部あるいは全部を無断で複写複製（撮影・デジタル化を含む）及び転載することは、法律上で認められた場合を除き、禁じられています。

乱丁、落丁本はお取り替えいたします。
ISBN978-4-255-15639-2

ちょっと手ごわい、でも効果絶大!
最強のリスニング強化マガジン

音声ダウンロード付き　毎月6日発売　定価1,263円(本体1,148円+税10%)

定期購読をお申し込みの方には本誌1号分無料ほか、特典多数。詳しくは下記ホームページへ。

英語が楽しく続けられる!

重大事件から日常のおもしろネタ、スターや著名人のインタビューなど、CNNの多彩なニュースを生の音声とともにお届けします。3段階ステップアップ方式で初めて学習する方も安心。どなたでも楽しく続けられて実践的な英語力が身につきます。

資格試験の強い味方!

ニュース英語に慣れれば、TOEIC®テストや英検のリスニング問題も楽に聞き取れるようになります。

CNN ENGLISH EXPRESS ホームページ

英語学習に役立つコンテンツが満載!

[本誌のホームページ] https://ee.asahipress.com/
[編集部のTwitter] https://twitter.com/asahipress_ee

朝日出版社　〒101-0065 東京都千代田区西神田 3-3-5　TEL 03-3263-3321

生きた英語でリスニング!

CNN ニュース・リスニング 2022[春夏]

1本30秒だから、聞きやすい!

電子書籍版付き
ダウンロード方式で提供

[30秒×3回聞き]方式で
世界標準の英語がだれでも聞き取れる!

- 羽生結弦、「氷上の王子」の座はゆずらない
- オックスフォード英語辞典にKカルチャー旋風
- 「母語」と「外国語」を犬も聞き分けている!…など

MP3音声・電子書籍版付き
(ダウンロード方式)
A5判 定価1100円(税込)

初級者からのニュース・リスニング
CNN Student News 2022 [夏秋]

音声アプリ+動画で、どんどん聞き取れる!

- レベル別に2種類の速度の音声を収録
- ニュース動画を字幕あり/なしで視聴できる

MP3・電子書籍版・
動画付き[オンライン提供]
A5判 定価1,320円(税込)

朝日出版社　〒101-0065 東京都千代田区西神田 3-3-5　TEL 03-3263-3321

GLobal ENglish Testing System

大学生向け団体受験用テスト

GLENTS Basic

グローバル英語力を測定
新時代のオンラインテスト

詳しくはWEBで！

https://www.asahipress.com/special/glents/organization/

銀行のセミナー・研修でお使いいただいています

Point 01
生の英語ニュースが素材

Point 02
場所を選ばず受験できるオンライン方式

Point 03
自動採点で結果をすぐに表示、
国際指標 CEFR にも対応

※画像はイメージです。

テストを受けてくださった学生のみなさまの反応

◇生の英語でのテストは非常に優位性があると思いました。
◇動画問題があるのが面白い！
◇将来海外に行くときに直接役立つと感じました。
◇音声を聞くことができる回数が1回のみだったので、
　真の「聞いて理解する力」を試されていると思いました。
◇多様な生の英語に慣れておく必要性を感じる良い経験となりました。

これからの大学生に求められる英語とは

企業が求める英語力はどんどん変化しています。これからの社会人は、違う文化を持つ人々と英語でしっかりコミュニケーションを取る必要があり、異文化に対する知識・理解を増やす必要があります。ですから、それらを身につけるために生の英語＝CNN GLENTS Basicで英語力を測り、CNNをはじめ様々なメディアで勉強することは非常に効果の高い学習法だと感じていますし、お勧めします。

鈴木武生氏

東京大学大学院総合文化研究科修了（言語情報科学専攻）。専門は英語、中国語、日本語の意味論。1991年にアジアユーロ言語研究所を設立。企業向けスキル研修、翻訳サービスなどを手掛ける。

受験料：大学生1人あたり 2,200 円（税込）　受験料は、受けていただく学生の人数によってご相談させていただきます。

株式会社 朝日出版社「CNN GLENTS」事務局　☎0120-181-202　✉glents_support@asahipress.com

® & © Cable News Network A WarnerMedia Company. All Rights Reserved.